Conten

The
FEMININE
CONNECTION:
Freeing the Female Psyche

Gayle Owens, Ph.D.

Feminine Connection: Freeing the Female Psyche

ISBN: 0-9744668-9-1

A Vivienne Book
Published by

TurnKey
press·

2525 W Anderson Lane, Suite 540
Austin, Texas 78757

Tel: 512.407.8876
Fax: 512.478.2117

E-mail: info@turnkeypress.com
Web: www.turnkeypress.com

To Morgan le Fay

"But Brigid is not a Christian saint," she thought.... "That is the Goddess as she is worshiped in Ireland. And I know it, and even if they think otherwise, these women know the power of the Immortal. Exile her as they may, she will prevail. The Goddess will never withdraw herself from mankind."

The Mists of Avalon, Marion Zimmer Bradley

Figure One: Vierge Ouvrante Closed

ACKNOWLEDGEMENTS

I am indebted in everyway to Carl G. Jung and Erich Neumann. My writing is based on their theory.

Case studies are composites of clients and are not based on any one actual client. My profound gratitude goes to all my clients; I have been privileged to witness their process.

Friends who are also psychotherapists read a very early version of this book and without their encouragement at that time I might never have continued writing. They are Betty Peterson, PhD, Tracey Spero Strucker, LPC, Jeannie Bunker, LMSW and Cynthia Watts, PhD.

Every effort was made to locate holders of copyrights. Grateful acknowledgement is made to the following for permission to use copyrighted material:

Quotes from *The Mists of Avalon* by Marion Zimmer Bradley, 1982. Reprinted by permission of the author and the author's agents, Scovil Chichak Galen Literary Agency, Inc.

The lines from *The Prophet* by Kahlil Gibran. Copyright 1923 by Kahlil Gibran and renewed 1951 by Administrators C.T.A. of Kahlil Gibran Estate and Mary G. Gibran. Used by permission of Alfred A. Knopf, a division of Random House, Inc.

The lines from "Turning the Wheel" from *A Wild Patience Has Taken Me This Far: Poems 1978-1981* by Adrienne Rich. Copyright © 1981 by Adrienne Rich. Used by permission of the author and W.W. Norton & Company, Inc.

Introduction

… when life unveils her holy face.[1]

We veil the feminine. Even though women have higher standing in our culture, we still bind the feminine in shame. Women and men are too enamored with the masculine principle and fear the feminine principle. Each of us plays our part in her veiling, even her burial, through our one-sidedness and our acceptance of dominant societal values.

Shrouding the feminine contributes to one's "psychological barrenness." After all, you as a woman are identified with the feminine, and thus identify with her, whether you want to or not. Long before you were capable of making conscious choices, by virtue of your anatomy, humankind knew you as one who belongs to the feminine archetype.

Thus, if you are not comfortable with the feminine, you are not comfortable with yourself. If you consider the feminine weak, stupid, silly, and irrelevant, you judge yourself at some level to be weak, stupid, silly, and irrelevant. If you oppress the feminine, you oppress yourself.

We as women and as a nation have much to celebrate in our quest for equality over the last 30 to 40 years. We have more social, economic, and political opportunity than ever before, but we have been co-opted by the patriarchy. We have closed our eyes to *feminine* equality, to the possibility of bringing the feminine into prominence in our lives and into our community. Since our reforms have only focused on change according to the masculine paradigm, the underlying cultural-psychological roots of our inequity, unhappiness, and subjugation have remained largely unrecognized and unremedied.

These unexamined cultural assumptions provoke humankind's rejection of the feminine and the resulting injury to women. The veil has been heavy, the burial deep.

We only know the caricature of the feminine that our culture has shown us. We don't know her as potency and puissance, Goddess and Great Mother, hinted at in prehistoric artifacts. We don't consciously know her as "Terrible Mother"— devouring and ensnaring, maddening enchantress, midwife of death.

Neither have we regarded her as the essential other half of human life. We have failed to notice that passion, "letting go," gentleness and intuition are wisdom qualities vital to human functioning. She, an undiscovered affluence within—the indispensable contrast and balance to the masculine. She, who can complete us.

Rending the veil reveals more and more of the depth of the feminine, until finally she is found to be our most excellent treasure. The feminine is the creative ground in which life itself manifests. On a physical level, her body—both the earth and the human—carries and nourishes new life. On a psychological level the unconscious gives birth to consciousness, and the continuing interplay between consciousness and unconsciousness is crucial if we are to have dynamic and vibrant minds. Hers is a formidable, dynamic, and boundless principle capable of bringing renewal to the psyche.

... the generating and nourishing, protective and transformative, feminine power of the unconscious ... intervenes, summoned or unsummoned, to save man (sic) and give direction to his life.[2]

... when life unveils her holy face.
But you are life and you are the veil.[3]

Chapter One

Woman's Identity

There is no light without shadow and no psychic wholeness without imperfection. To round itself out, life calls not for perfection but for completeness;

C. G. Jung, 1968[1]

The feminine—an archetype, the universal human pattern for the other half, the half not masculine—is the essence of every woman. Yet in spite of her enormous significance, she is a stranger to us. We live in a culture built and sustained by masculine ideals. Fearing the feminine as a threat to its continued dominance, the masculine value system strives to make the feminine invisible. Along with belittlement and scorn, most of what is feminine goes unrecognized, for what is not conscious in people's minds is not seen as a threat.

Why should we care? Why should we be concerned about something as abstract as cultural values? Because women have been identified with this "outcast"—the feminine—since the beginning of civilization. When she is unexamined, unknown, and rejected, we hide part of who we are from ourselves.

Our identification with her has its origins in biology, because in the beginning, biology distinguished female from male. Women received men's penis and sperm into their bodies. Blood flowed from women. Sometimes the blood stopped for a while, and women gave birth to babies that they nourished with milk from their breasts.

These biological functions associated females with mystery, receptivity, incubation, nourishment, life, and other qualities that have since become known as feminine. Whether we like it or not, women's identity is feminine—as feminine has been culturally defined—because our biology has interacted with the history of civilization to make it so.

Because we are identified with her, the culture's devaluation of her is the underpinning for our lack of self-esteem. My experience as a clinician, researcher and woman convinces me that most women struggle with their self-esteem. Poor self-esteem manifests itself as a persistent sense of inadequacy. Women don't like and accept themselves. Some of us are blatant misogynists. Some women seem to preface every act by apologizing for being. Even women who appear to be most confident will admit they fake it at times and really don't believe in themselves.

We reject the feminine, harming ourselves over and over again without even knowing it, because the injury has become the norm. But when we open our eyes, we see that females, from their day of birth, are thrust into a world that fosters a sense of inferiority.

Examples range from more parents wishing for a boy than for a girl; to teachers rewarding and encouraging boys more than girls to be curious and to answer questions in class; to women who spend an inordinate part of their lives searching for a husband because they think they're not enough without a man; to women still being paid less than their male counterparts for the same jobs.

Even though much of the blatant discrimination against women has been eliminated over the decades, sadly, many more subtly unequal situations and pejorative attitudes toward women remain. Little girls are regularly immersed in an environment (not just from their families, but from the media, day care, schools, churches, adults in their community and peers) that teaches them that the feminine and, by association, themselves, are not as worthwhile as the masculine and boys. When the masculine is the standard for the culture, girls are deviant. Even the language we speak grammatically subsumes feminine under the masculine.[2]

The Black Woman

I encountered the Black woman, the repressed feminine, in a dream several years ago:

> I and all the other women in a large auditorium are enthralled by the dance of two ballerinas. Then, an elderly black woman, an African American, arrives at the back of the auditorium, compelling us with her presence. The musicians and the dancers stop to see her, all of us bending toward her. She, of breathtaking nobility and dignity. We stand in reverence as she makes her way to her seat.

An image of an elderly black woman is a precise personification of our cultural view of the feminine. Our culture defines a dark-skinned woman—especially an African American—as inferior. The Black woman, depicting the feminine, represents what has been rejected and oppressed in our "dance of life"—in our culture and in our psyches. The feminine resides in our unconscious and on the fringes of our culture, waiting for recognition and emancipation.

In the dream, we felt reverence, respect and adoration for a woman—an elderly black woman—the feminine. Consider the possibility of having such esteem for yourself for no other reason than because you are a woman. What might this self-respect mean for your life, for your children, and for your community?

After years of women striving for equality, it is disappointing that, on the whole, women do not esteem themselves, but have moved further away from being authentic. In our focus on external equality, we have neglected, even rejected, our feminine selves. We have little appreciation for our femininity, our relation to the feminine. At times we are even ashamed of our gender. Yet it is a given that women and men admire men simply for their connection to the masculine, for their masculinity. The feminist prescription for success has been to downplay our femininity while doing our best to heighten our masculine qualities.

Feminists haven't and can't bring the feminine to the fore because they, too, operate within the patriarchal mindset. Over the centuries, this patriarchal domination has reduced the feminine to a caricature in our minds. If our image of her is big breasts, stilettos, fuzzy thinking, and weakness, then this trivial portrayal assures that we will not want to claim her.

And not claiming her perpetuates the trouble. Regardless of what we may have achieved in the world—position, status, power—we are set up to feel inferior as human beings. From the day of our birth, our culture subtly and blatantly teaches us to admire the masculine while ignoring the redeeming and constructive qualities of the feminine. Some communities and families go even further and actively teach us not to like the feminine (and, by association, femininity)—perhaps even to fear and detest her. How could we not be harmed by these attitudes? Our view of ourselves, which is our foundation for self-esteem and self-love, is undermined.

No War of the Sexes

Lest I am misunderstood, my point is not to make the feminine dominant in your psyche or in your community; rather, it is to stress mutuality. It is not about conflict, but about peace. The Western way of thinking—analyzing, comparing, and assigning cause and effect—often leads to win-lose results. But living out the feminine can't be done at the expense of the masculine principle or of men. The intention is to bring together the masculine and the feminine in consciousness. Some have suggested that this mutuality, this unity, is the next step in the evolution of consciousness.[3] Consciousness that is inclusive of the feminine could lead to personal renewal and transformation of our society. Metaphorically, we are in need of resurrecting the goddesses who have been shrouded and buried. Not to defeat the god, as our competitive culture would presume, but to fulfill the prophecy:

The wolf shall dwell with the lamb,
and the leopard shall lie down with the kid,
and the calf and the lion and the fatling together....[4]

The Shrouded Feminine

Women who are successful by today's standards are successful because they have adopted the masculine standard. Besides showing they can be just as good real estate agents, bankers, farmers and technicians as men, they are proudly managing complex lives. They are engaging in romantic relationships, managing a household, acting as caretakers for children or elderly parents, and performing responsible jobs—all at the same time. Vowing not to live unfulfilled as did their mothers and grandmothers, they have learned to be as smart, action-oriented and as fast as their male friends.

Many of these women grew up in families that lived out rigid sex roles. Dad earned the money and made the decisions, while Mom's care of the home, children, and husband was not valued. The fact that these sex roles existed points to how lifeless and devalued our view of the feminine had become. The definition of feminine in the 1950s sank to a new low as it came to mean weak, silly, childlike—a plaything, a man's adjunct. (I am aware, as are you, no doubt, that many women and men still adhere to these sex roles today, even when the woman works outside of the home.)

Unfortunately, Western culture's derogatory view of the feminine is much older and even more entrenched than the values of the 1950s. Our oldest and best-known literature, the Bible, defines the feminine in Genesis with the introduction of Eve, first woman. In one of the creation stories, Eve is an afterthought—taken from man's rib to be his helpmate. Then she is blamed for her husband's, indeed, all of mankind's, fall from grace. She is portrayed as evil, cunning and secondary to Adam. God addresses her, for all of humankind to hear: "… your husband, and he shall rule over you."[5]

Lest people might stray from this view, Tertullian, an influential early Christian writer and father of the church, wrote to women in the second century A.D.:

> And do you not know that you are an Eve? The sentence of God on this sex of yours lives in this age; the guilt must of necessity live too. You are the devil's gateway … the first deserter of the divine law; you are she who persuaded him whom the devil was not valiant enough to attack. You destroyed so easily God's image, man. On account of your desert—that is, death, even the Son of God had to die.[6]

Genesis personified woman as the original sinner. In the 1950s she was portrayed as a silly child in a woman's body. Between these times is a long history of viewing the feminine with contempt and shame.[7] Particularly noteworthy is the period from the 1300s to the 1600s when millions of women were burned as witches. Women who were different were targets of these burnings, including those with disabilities; women who were exceptionally pretty or had sexually aroused a man; women who were outspoken, or those who were thought to have some kind of power.[8]

Life Stance

Oppression, violence, slavery, and rigid sex roles characterize women's history. It is no wonder women's survival instinct kicks in as they form attitudes about their life stance. One attitude or "script" for women—its potency proportional to its inaccessibility to the conscious mind—is to go along with the culture. Identify with and live out society's view of the feminine and of women as inferior beings—or perhaps even as victims.

A second life stance is a solution many baby boomers have taken on: women have thrown the feminine aside with a conscious decision to adopt the masculine, focusing on developing masculine qualities. (Though I am presenting the two life positions in their extremes, they are not necessarily mutually exclusive.)

Self-denigration

Thanks to women's liberation and the feminist movement, over the last 40 years we have seen the ambitious, achievement-oriented masculine energy residing within women's psyches become activated in large measure. Assuredly, the emergence of the masculine has had its positive benefits as women have made significant economic and social strides. But either stance—

women living as subordinates to men or women living out the masculine and ignoring or repudiating the feminine—ends in self-denigration. Women who assign themselves to secondary personhood have internalized the disparagement of society. Women who reject the feminine to better embrace the masculine dislike the primary core of themselves.

One way this rejection manifests itself on the outside is in how women feel about their bodies. So many women dislike their bodies that we have come to accept body-hatred as the norm for women. Perhaps women are callous toward their bodies because the female body does not behave like the standard—the male body. Or do women feel the same toward their bodies as they do towards the feminine that it "embodies"?

We "successful" women notice our lack of fulfillment and unease and wonder what's wrong. We sense that we have somehow failed, or are we being exploited? We see the poor choices we've made in partners. We long to share an intimate relationship, yet we don't know how. Some of us have eating disorders and hide in the unconsciousness of our addiction. Some of us stay exhaustively busy so we won't have to feel. Others are plagued by depression. Some of us feel brittle, suspecting we fit the classic definition of bitch. But we shrug our shoulders, believing being a bitch is the price we must pay to make it in a man's world. Intuitively, we know something is missing from our lives, but we never suspect it could be ourselves.

My own uneasiness, along with my awareness of other women's disappointment and sorrow, finally prompted me to pay attention to what I had ignored and rejected. Over several years I had haunting, guilt-provoking dreams about little girls, identified as my daughter, whom I was neglecting. To my horror, I would forget her, leaving her outside, exposed to the cold and rain. In other dreams, I would suddenly realize I had not fed her for days, or that she would be dressed in her one tattered, too-small dress, because I had, again, failed to buy her clothes.

These dreams reflected my thoughtless attitude toward the feminine. The remorse they roused tore at me. They told me I would not find peace until I stopped neglecting her; indeed, until I properly clothed and fed her and brought her in, out of the cold, and into my life.

My dreams were my path to the feminine. Other women have discovered her through self-expression: writing, drawing, painting, or sculpture. Some seek her through their relationships with other women. Jean Shinoda Bolen speaks of awakening to the feminine through the experience of childbirth.[9] Leslie Shore writes of finding her through contact with the earth and nature.[10]

Honoring the Feminine

What would it mean if the feminine were honored? Primarily, we would be proud to be female. Our female body and its sexuality, maternal capacity, and menstruation would be celebrated. (Contrast this with societies who banish women from the community during their menstrual flow.) We would place a higher value on our character than on our appearance because society's regard for us would go beyond the superficiality of "tits and ass." Women and men would dignify women's history, women's traditions and women's contributions.

Can you imagine how affirming the feminine would change the way girls are raised? Baby girls would be as welcome at birth as baby boys. Little girls would glory in their gender and their bodies. Parents and teachers would encourage girls as much as they encourage boys. Little girls would *want* to grow up to be "just like Mom." The menarche would be celebrated. Girls with aptitudes in science and math would continue to excel in those subjects in junior high, high school and college. Teenage girls would devote more energy toward developing their own identities and less energy toward getting a boyfriend. They would be less likely to allow sexual contact when they were not prepared for the consequences. Teenagers (and women) who liked themselves would choose healthy, responsible and loving partners.

At long last, women's egos would be strengthened, resulting in less victim identity and dependency. Women who liked themselves would have nothing less than egalitarian relationships and respectful treatment in all aspects of their lives.

Revering the feminine has remarkable ramifications for our society. With feminine values in balance with masculine values, we would be truly compassionate—and not just because it makes good sense politically or economically to appear compassionate. We would care as much about people's welfare as we do about making money or being in power.

A society that has lost its connection to the feminine has also lost its connection to nature, to heaven and to earth. We no longer know how to nurture our environment, so we go about destroying our ecology, as well as each other. Restoring the feminine could help to heal our personal connection with the trees, oceans, and mountains. We would recognize our obligation and interrelationship with Mother Earth.

They live in wisdom who see themselves in all and all in them,
Bhagavad Gita[11]

Chapter Two

Who is She?

So long as you want her faceless, without smell
Or voice ...
She is kept helpless and conventional
her true power routed backward
into the past, we cannot touch or name her
and, barred from participation by those who need her
she stifles in unspeakable loneliness.

Adrienne Rich, 1981[1]

The feminine is an archetypal idea, a thousand different images, an infinite concept. Although we can experience her, we can never find the right words to describe her. As an archetype, she is an idea *en potentia*, a universal human pattern. Eve, Sophia, the Great Goddess, Jezebel, Venus, the Virgin Mary, Demeter, and Persephone each symbolize an aspect of the feminine.

Carl Jung popularized the notion of each human psyche carrying the original patterns (archetypes) for the feminine and for the masculine.[2] But thousands of years earlier, the Taoists (ancient Chinese philosophers) also recognized the feminine and her counterpart, naming her Yin. Yin and Yang are Taoist terms for the principles of nature that together form all there is: the whole. (See Figure Two for the Taoist's symbolic rendering of

Yin and Yang, depicting their interdependence. The light [Yang] fades into the dark [Yin]; the dark fades into the light. At the center of the dark is the light; at the center of the light is the dark. The circle is complete only because both Yin and Yang are present.)

Yin and Yang

Yin is "the cloudy, the overcast."[3] It is depicted by the earth, the feminine, the dark, the moist, the receptive. Yin is the principle of surrender, completion, modesty, relatedness, letting events unfold as they are meant to be in their own time.[4]

Yang, the other half of the Chinese symbol for wholeness, is "banners waving in the sun, something shone upon or bright."[5] It is the heaven, the sky, the masculine, the bright, the dry, the thruster. Yang is the principle of activity, assertiveness, perfection, achievement, taking charge and making events happen.[6]

The mythologist Joseph Campbell suggested some descriptions that complement the Taoists' thinking:

> The left, the side of the heart, the shield side, has been symbolic, traditionally and everywhere, of feeling, mercy and love, vulnerability and defenselessness, the feminine virtues and dangers: mothering and seduction, the tidal powers of the moon and substances of the body, the rhythms of the seasons: gestation, birth, nourishment, and fosterage; yet equally malice, and revenge, unreason, dark and terrible wrath, black magic, poisons, sorcery, and delusions; but also fair enchantment, beauty, rapture, and bliss.
>
> And the right, thereby, is of the male: action, weapons, hero-deeds, protection, brute force, and both cruel and benevolent justice; the masculine virtues and dangers: egoism and aggression, lucid luminous reason, sunlike

Figure Two: Yin Yang

creative power, but also cold unfeeling malice, abstract spirituality, blind courage, theoretical dedication, sober, unplayful moral force.[7]

Contrast Campbell's expansive definition of the feminine archetype with your idea of the feminine self in our culture. When I ask women what they think of when I say "feminine," their reply is almost always "weak." This is only the beginning of the misunderstandings that surround what it means to be feminine.

Female Gender

For example, the feminine is not synonymous with the female gender, although the female has certainly been identified with her throughout the ages. Female is a biological term, defining those humans of the sex who can become pregnant and give birth.[8] In actuality, some men may express more of the feminine than do some women.

Sex Roles

Sex roles, or gender roles, also should not be confused with the feminine. Sex roles are clusters of activities society assigns to people based on their sex. For example, "housewife" is a role that is still fairly strong in our society. "Parent" is another role more heavily assigned to women than to men. Traditionally, nurses and secretaries have been women, and truck drivers and coaches have been men. But we can assume nothing about a woman's expression of the masculine or feminine based on whether she is a housewife or an engineer.

Sexual Orientation

Expressing the feminine or the masculine is also not tied to sexual orientation. Lesbians are not lesbians because they are "too" masculine, nor because they are "too" feminine.

History of the Feminine: The Matriarchy

Given this cultural vagueness and ambiguity, the question becomes how did the feminine become marginalized? Eric Neumann, a disciple of Carl Jung, theorized that she was buried under layer upon layer of civilization's evolution. At the beginning of human culture, the instinctual, unconscious feminine principle was dominant. It was the consciousness of the Great Goddess, the Primordial Mother; from this base rose a matriarchal society.[9]

As it is with a baby, so it was for the earliest humans. A baby lives in a contained instinctual world of feelings and sensations. She is unconscious in the sense that she has no boundaries around her self; she makes no distinction between her self and other, between "I" and "not I." The baby is thus totally dependent on her surroundings.[10]

In the matriarchal society, people lived in small tribes or clans; their identities were contained within their groups. Certainly, they depended on Mother Earth for their survival. Our patriarchal mind assumes a matriarchal society would give females higher status than males, making males servants. But the matriarchy was not the opposite of the patriarchy. It did not oppress males. In the matriarchy, females and males were believed to be of equal importance to the family and to the tribe.[11]

Rise of the Masculine Consciousness

The state of unity of primitive humans was countered by a push for separation, for individual identity—just as the baby pushes her mother away, crawling across the floor to explore her colorful toys. Early humans began to act on their environment by hunting, gathering, and building structures. Such activity was the beginning of the development of the ego, along with the parallel development of the patriarchy. Patriarchal or masculine consciousness is characterized by increasing differentiation from one's surroundings, leading to individual identity. Analytical thinking and objectivity are both the seeds and fruits of masculine consciousness. The result for humans has been an ever-expanding consciousness as the ego has been continually fortified throughout the ages.[12]

Thus, consciousness—ego functioning or differentiation—was and is a masculine function. Of course, the development of the ego has occurred within women just as it has within men through the ages. In humanity, for both men and women, the evolutionary task was the expansion of consciousness.

The Great Goddess

According to Neumann, as (masculine) consciousness began to develop and dominate, monumental changes occurred to the matriarchy and the feminine. In the matriarchal era, the Great Goddess was understood to contain the polar opposites—"Good Mother" and "Terrible Mother." Good Mother was the archetype of the ideal universal mother. She was creator of life: ever-present, ever-nurturing, always loving, forever available. Her breasts were full of milk that continuously flowed to her children.[13]

The Terrible Mother was too much or too little. She suffocated her children, crippled their independence, starved, or ignored them. Her breasts were dry. Early humans with fledgling egos were terrified of her ability to pull them back into an unconscious state. Euripides' Medea was such a woman, murdering her own children to cause suffering for her husband, their father. Adding to her horrific reputation, the Terrible Mother was known as the usher for death. Indeed, at death, humans literally went back to Terrible Mother since they were buried in the earth. While the womb stood for Good Mother, the tomb stood for Terrible Mother.[14]

Neumann's theory is that as the patriarchy developed, humans repressed the powerfulness of the Mothers, eventually virtually wiping them out of human consciousness.[15] With this repression, the feminine archetype became an anemic whisper of who she had been; evil lingered, but the potency was gone. By fundamentally losing the dark side of the archetype, the feminine lost vitality, independence, sexuality, her impressive display of power. Lost was the respect that comes from being a force with which to be reckoned. She was no longer revered and feared, as were the male gods. Now, she would be inferior to the masculine.

Innana

The ancient Sumerian goddess Innana was one embodiment of the Great Goddess (including the Terrible Mother). Innana represented a primitive but wholeness pattern of the feminine, going beyond the maternal. She combined "… earth and sky, matter and spirit, vessel and light, earthly bounty and heavenly guidance."[16] She was also the goddess of war and described in one hymn as "… all-devouring in … power … attacking like the attacking storm, having an awesome face and angry heart, and she sings with abandoned delight of her own glory and prowess."[17]

Inanna, "equally passionately … is goddess of sexual love."[18] In these verses, Inanna is speaking to her lover:

My vulva, the horn, the boat of heaven, is full of eagerness like the young moon.
My untilled land lies fallow.
As for me, Inanna, who will plow my vulva?
Who will plow my high field?
Who will plow my wet ground?
As for me, the young woman, who will station the ox there?
Who will plow my vulva?[19]

Now contrast Inanna with her patriarchal replacement, the Virgin Mary in the Western Protestant tradition. Mary is made homely. She is bloodless. She has no power. She is sweetness, light, purity, innocence. She isn't even sullied by earthly lust or sex, having been conceived and herself conceiving from some sort of purity through the Holy Spirit. What do we learn from Mary? The Madonna-Whore dilemma: We are to be mothers, but we shouldn't like sex or our own lives. Mary is the "nice woman" our culture wants us to emulate.

Evil and Weak

Two concepts that have been disastrous for the feminine and women converged with the dawn of the patriarchy. The first is that the feminine (and therefore woman) is evil. She is the originator of sin and makes the human male do evil things. The second is that the feminine (and therefore woman) is weak. Her only acceptable role is mother, and her function is as a vessel that incubates and nurtures. She must associate with a male for strength because she has no efficacy, no power and no energy of her own. What a perfect setup to perpetuate masculine dominance—women believing they are both evil and powerless!

By the way, if there's any doubt our culture believes feminine means "weak," look up the word in a dictionary. My latest dictionary, published in 1997, lists the second definition as "having qualities regarded as characteristic of women and girls, as gentleness, *weakness*, delicacy, modesty, etc.; womanly."[20]

Women who feel guilty or fearful about owning their personal authority carry this legacy of "making nice." They believe it's wrong to express their opinions, especially to disagree. The possibility that others will be angry is always in the back of their minds. Claiming self-efficacy can lead to rejection—by their peers, their bosses, their families, or by the men they love. Do you find yourself denying your anger? Are you sometimes passive when others behave badly toward you? Do you sometimes turn your anger into tears and hurt instead? Remember the Virgin Mary and how her power has been shoved into the dark. If this describes your behavior, besides abandoning your power, you are also abandoning your capacity to be real, to be heard.

Battered women especially play out this evil-nice (nice equals powerless) legacy. They blame themselves for the abuse. Somehow they believe they deserve it or are responsible for the actions of their abuser. Then they believe they must stay in the relationship because they cannot survive outside of it.

Many women don't identify themselves as a feminist for the same reasons they don't display anger or disagreement. The definition of a feminist is simply one who believes women should have the same right to self-determination and self-respect as men. But women claiming this identity imply personal power and responsibility, thereby bringing about anger and threats from society.

Summing Up

In terms of the patriarchy and the feminine, Neumann suggested that the suppression of the matriarchal by a patriarchal epoch was a universal and necessary phenomenon in the history of humankind. He described the rise of patriarchy as the evolutionary push needed for the development of the ego, and thus consciousness. But before his death, he warned that the patriarchy and the developed ego were not to be the end point of human consciousness. He was disturbed by the over-emphasis on analytical thinking, the scientific method, the use of logic, and the subsequent devaluation of the unconscious and the feminine. He warned that extreme ego consciousness was leading to meaningless lives, body alienation, hatred of life, and world negation.[21]

Chapter Three

The Patriarchy and the Unconscious

If combat means living in a ditch, females have biological problems staying in a ditch for 30 days because they get infections and they don't have upper body strength.

Newt Gingrich, 1995[1]

If woman alone had suffered under these mistaken traditions, if she could have borne the evil by herself, it would have been less pitiful, but her brother man, in the laws he created and ignorantly worshiped, has suffered with her. He has lost her highest help; he has crippled the intelligence he needed; he has belittled the very source of his own being and dwarfed the image of his Maker.

Clara Barton, 1902[2]

Accompanying the development of the patriarchy was the attitude that males were superior to females. Superior males were entitled to determine women's lives.[3] In my home state of Texas, married women could not control their own property or run a business without their husbands' consent until 1967. I was shocked when I discovered this law and realized that it had actually applied to me, since I had been married in Texas in 1964. I would have needed my husband's consent to file a lawsuit, and, had he been so inclined, he could have instructed the bank not to honor my checks written out of my own money.[4]

The Hammurabic laws from about 1750 B.C., the predecessors of our current laws, expose the patriarchy's proprietary attitude toward women. Their laws against rape incorporated the principle that the injured party was the husband or the father of the raped woman, not the woman raped. These laws show that women were viewed as equivalents of breeding mares: their usefulness came from procreation. Therefore it was the husband's or father's property that was damaged if the woman was "spoiled" for procreation. Women were required to prove they had resisted rape by struggling or shouting, or they were considered the guilty party. If a married man raped a virgin, the father of the virgin could take the rapist's wife and use her sexually at his discretion, even turning her into a prostitute. The raped virgin would be required to marry the man who had raped her.[5]

Recently, Peruvian legislators were debating whether to overthrow a law in their country allowing a rapist to escape punishment if he offers to marry his victim and she agrees. Also, the law allows all the perpetrators in a gang rape to go free if one of the co-defendants agrees to marry the woman who was raped. It is said that marriage is an acceptable response to rape in Peru because women often feel they have lost their value once they have lost their virginity.[6] Likewise in many states in Mexico, the law requires the girl or woman to first prove she is "chaste and pure" before she can accuse an adult man of rape. And statutory rape charges will be dropped if the rapist agrees to marry his victim.[7]

The same unimaginable circumstances also applied to mental health. For example, an Illinois law, passed in 1851, provided that married women and infants could be entered or detained in the Illinois State Hospital for the Insane on the request of the husband of the woman or the guardian of the infant, without the evidence of insanity required in other cases. The legal basis for this law was the principle of coverture: the very being or legal existence of a married woman was suspended during the marriage and given to her husband.[8]

Even some of the personality tests used during the 1960s and 1970s to measure mental health showed women to be maladjusted if they weren't living out the traditional roles. One of the most popular of these personality tests, the MMPI, suggested pathology because, when I took it, I was single, 30ish and a graduate school student. Almost any woman professional, particularly if she was in the sciences, would have been found "deviant" by the MMPI. (This test was eventually revised.)

Besides the evolutionary push for increased consciousness, the patriarchal attitude toward the feminine (and women) has been attributed to biological, social, economic, and political reasons. Harriet Lerner, in *The Creation of the Patriarchy*,[9] provides a satisfying discussion of these factors, which she shows to be complicated, subtle, obvious, unknown, and inexplicable. But, regardless of whether we can ever satisfactorily explain why the patriarchy came about, several historical facts are indisputable: As the patriarchy and the status of men rose, the feminine and the status of women declined. As consciousness became dominant, unconscious was disregarded, even avoided.

The Wisdom of the Unconscious

The wisdom of the unconscious? The hidden treasure? What's so consequential about the unconscious? When we think of the unconscious, we usually imagine the *personal* unconscious, the psychic repository for all that we have experienced, but then have forgotten, repressed, or suppressed. And it probably seems obvious that recalling and processing these contents can help us overcome interpersonal or performance problems. But Dr. Jung introduced the idea that our unconscious reaches far beyond its relatively modest personal face:

> Our personal psychology is just a thin skin, a ripple on the ocean of collective psychology. The powerful factor, the factor which changes our whole life, which changes the surface of our known world, which makes history, is collective psychology, and collective psychology moves according to laws entirely different from those of our consciousness.[10]

When we really pay attention, we notice that the primary influence for many ideas, feelings, attitudes, and behaviors comes from the collective unconscious. One of the ways the collective unconscious serves the conscious personality is through the *law of compensation*, a valuable tool for psychological growth. The collective unconscious compensates for conscious views that may be too one-sided or just plain false through dreams and visions, by causing actions and reactions, and by causing feelings. For example, the compensation function was in action when I was being prodded by my dreams to change my mind about what was feminine.

My favorite example of a compensatory dream is one Dr. Jung told about himself. He was having a difficult analysis with a patient, but didn't know why. Then he dreamt that he saw her at some height above him and, to see her properly, he had to bend his head far back. When he woke, he even had a crick in his neck. He says he immediately realized that if in the dream he had to look up to the patient, in reality, he had probably been looking down on her. He shared his realization with the patient the next time they were together, and the analysis improved as a result.[11]

Dr. Jung was fond of saying that each of us has within our psyche a Wise One with two million years of experience.[12] By this metaphor, he was referring to the organizing principle of the human psyche that exists at the center of the collective unconscious: the Self. (The Self is written with a capital "S" to distinguish it from our subjective sense of self, or ego.) The Self's function is constructive and forward-looking. The law of compensation is one way we see the Self operating. The Self's mission is transformative—to move the personality toward individuation—toward becoming uniquely and fully authentic as a human being.

The transformative aspect of the collective unconscious is analogous to woman's experience of pregnancy and birth. (She cooperates with a part of nature she cannot control or intellectually explain to produce life.) The transformative function sets the personality in motion, producing growth, generation, creativity, and, ultimately, individuation.[13] "It is not I who create myself, rather I happen to myself," Jung summarizes pithily.[14]

Neumann wrote of the collective unconscious and the Self, saying that:

> All art, religion, science, and technology, everything that has ever been done, spoken, or thought, has its origin in this creative center. The self-generating power of the soul is man's(sic) true and final secret, by virtue of which he is made in the likeness of God the creator and distinguished from all other living things.[15]

Creativity and renewal come from engaging the unconscious, Neumann reminded us. He was disturbed that the reality of the soul and the unconscious were neglected by the dominant society. The masculine principle of consciousness had gone too far, he warned, creating a dangerous situation for the psychological health of humans. The masculine consciousness, "which desires permanence and not change, eternity and not transformation, law and not creative spontaneity, 'discriminates' against the Great Goddess and turns her into a demon."[16]

Neumann was referring to the transformative character of the collective unconscious when he urged us to find and redeem our feminine. Then we would have the highest treasure of all: "... male consciousness totally overlooks the hidden spiritual aspect of the feminine principle, which through spiritual transformation exalts earthly man to a higher meaning."[17]

Everyone's Treasure

Neumann was sensitive to the potential. He believed a revolution was waiting to take place in the psyches of women and men when humans' acknowledge and redeem their feminine. The lost wisdom, now terribly needed, is that the unconscious, identified with the feminine, and also the function of the unconscious—also identified with the feminine—is everyone's treasure house.

Will We Be Saved?

In the last two chapters, we have come full circle with our discussion of the feminine and the unconscious. The earliest humans lived in an unconscious state that was identified with the feminine and the matriarchy. Then they began striving for consciousness—a monumental masculine activity that has made us who we are as humans today. Greater consciousness has brought us the patriarchy and the achievements of Western civilization.

The unconscious was initially a threat to a fledgling consciousness. Thus it was feared and degraded, as was the feminine with which it was identified. But too much attention to our rational mind is now cause for trepidation. Too much consciousness is causing us to destroy our land and sky, our communities, our families, our bodies, and our souls.

We are at a threshold—or is it a precipice? Will we integrate and balance the conscious and the unconscious? Will we use the transforming power of the unconscious and the feminine as a partner to conscious activity and the masculine?

A small island of consciousness had much to fear from the boundless ocean of the unconscious, but now consciousness is a well-developed and vast continent. Consciousness as a continent is poisoning its own water and air, decimating its trees, thirsting on and depleting its rich soil. As it drifts toward becoming an uninhabitable desert, it is once more in danger of engulfment by the ocean of unconscious, but now because of its own arrogance. In failing to recognize its creator, it refuses its revival.

Vierge Ouvrante

The two statues of the *Vierge Ouvrante*, (Figure One, page 5 and Figure Three, page 116) picture what Dr. Neumann and I have tried to impart with words. The *Vierge Ouvrante Closed* shows Mary (the feminine) holding her baby (masculine, consciousness). The human mother has given birth to the divine child, signifying a transcendent advance for humankind—a new state of consciousness. This statue thus depicts the traditional meaning of Jesus' birth and the rise of the patriarchy.[18]

But once the Vierge Ouvrante is opened, our understanding shifts. We discover the father god along with the son god sitting on the lap of the Great Goddess (Mother Nature). Here, in contradiction to New Testament text, Mary is revealed in the old images of the past: as the Great Goddess of Life and Death; Queen of Heaven, Earth, and the Underworld; Sophia. The source of father and son is the collective unconscious. They do not exist apart from her. Although they are different from her, it is she who has created them and who will continue to infuse them through her transformative function.

From the masculine conscious come the laws of civilization, humans' enterprise since we began our struggle to live in the world. But from the feminine collective unconscious come the laws of nature and life.[19] "Rational truths are not the last word, there are also irrational ones."[20] No matter our intellect, our ego strength, our scientific knowledge, our legal structures, we are superseded by nature, by human nature, by Mother Earth, by the giver of forms. We need her. We must remember her, turn toward her, be in relationship with her.

Chapter Four

What Do Women Want?

What is it that women most desire, above all else?
King Arthur, 14th Century[1]

A Myth of Sir Gawain, from The Arthur Legends[2]

Sir Gromer, a fearsome knight of the northern lands, accosted King Arthur one day while he was out hunting alone. As was the custom of that time Sir Gromer sought revenge from Arthur because he had been caught poaching on Sir Gromer's land as a young boy. But on this particular day Sir Gromer spared Arthur, giving him a chance to save his life by meeting him in a year at the same spot with the answer to the question: "What is it that women most desire, above all else?" If Arthur found the correct answer to this question his life would be spared. If not, Sir Gromer would kill him.

During the next year King Arthur and his knights, including Sir Gawain, his nephew, collected answers from one end of the kingdom to the other. Yet as the anniversary grew near, Arthur was worried that none of the answers had the ring of truth.

A few days before he was to meet Sir Gromer, Arthur encountered a grotesque hag at a grove of great oaks. She was ugly, had but one tooth, gave forth a stench that would sicken a goat, made obscene sounds, and was humpbacked—in short, the most loathsome creature he had ever seen.

The woman told Arthur she knew he was about to meet her stepbrother, Sir Gromer, and that she alone could tell him the correct answer to save his life. But what a price to pay for the answer. She would tell Arthur, but only if Sir Gawain would marry her. Arthur was shocked, crying out that what she asked was impossible.

When Arthur returned home that evening, he looked so pale and shaken that Gawain asked him what was wrong. Arthur resisted telling him, but eventually spoke of the bargain the hag had proposed. Gawain was delighted he would be able to save Arthur's life, finally persuading Arthur to take him to the grove of oak trees the next day to meet the woman. The marriage was agreed upon, provided the woman's answer was correct.

The following day Arthur rode out alone to meet Sir Gromer. Arthur first tried all of his other answers, but then, just as Sir Gromer was lifting his sword to kill Arthur, Arthur added, "I have one more answer. What a woman desires above all else is the power of sovereignty—the right to exercise her own will." Sir Gromer was angry when he heard this answer, knowing his stepsister must have supplied it, and he ran off into the forest.

Gawain held to his promise, marrying the hag that very day. All of Arthur's court was present. Gawain was courteous, gentle, and respectful. The old witch exhibited her worst manners by wolfing the food from her plate without the aid of utensils, while emitting hideous noises and smells. Never before or since had the court of Arthur been subject to so much strain. But courtesy prevailed, and the wedding was accomplished.

Gawain and his bride retired to their chambers. Gawain prepared for the wedding bed, waiting for the hag to join him. But to his astonishment, she appeared as the loveliest maiden a man could ever wish to see. Gawain, in his amazement, asked what had happened. The maiden answered that because Gawain had been courteous to her, she would show him her grotesque aspect half the time and her gracious side the other half of the time.

"And which do you choose for the day and which for the night?" she asked him. Would he wish her to be a maiden during the day with his friends and in King Arthur's court, keeping the ugliness for him alone at night? Or would he wish her to save her loveliness for him at night when they were together and intimate?

Gawain thought for a minute, then knelt before her, touching her hand, and told her it was her choice to make. He said he would willingly support whatever she chose. At this, she announced she would be a fair damsel to him both day and night, since he had given her the respect to exercise her own free will.

Lessons

The lessons of this myth speak to us on at least two different levels. First, women can identify with the desire, indeed, their own personal struggle, to have sovereignty over their lives and to make decisions for themselves.

On the second level, it speaks about the feminine archetype. The culture does its best to turn the feminine into a non-entity or a hag. Unlike Sir Gawain, we have not been courteous, gentle, or respectful to the feminine archetype, allowing her to express herself through us. But what happens when this feminine energy is repressed for eons?

Jung told us:

Archetypes were, and still are, living psychic forces that demand to be taken seriously, and they have a strange way of making sure of their effect … they are the infallible causes of neurotic and even psychotic disorders, behaving exactly like neglected or maltreated physical organs or organic functional systems.[3]

Each of us who represses the feminine carries a hag around inside, and she rages against her lack of sovereignty. Moreover, because she embodies the anger and self-destruction that comes from our self-oppression, she is every bit as ugly as Sir Gawain's hag. She is the image of our own self-hatred. It is right for us to fear her, for if we continue to ignore her, she has the potential to destroy us. (If you would like to communicate with your hag, turn to the Appendix.)

Sir Gaiwain would not dominate the feminine in the Arthurian myth. Yet we all know many ways the feminine principle is dominated. We see this attitude played out in women's dislike, even shame, of their bodies. A survey found that 53 percent of 13-year-old American girls and 78 percent of 17-year-old girls were dissatisfied with their bodies.[4] Women have a long tradition of preferring to look good rather than to feel good. Consider corsets, clip on earrings, Wonderbras, girdles, Botox and Retin-A. Patricia Lynn Reilly remarks: "In desperation women ask, 'Why is it that men wake up in the morning and are enough? Why is it that we wake up and must add to our faces, adorn our bodies, and cover our scents and roundness in order to be enough—and we still fall short?'"[5]

Women who cram their bodies into high-heeled, pointy-toed shoes and push-up brassieres while coping with a miniskirt want to be seen as sex objects. They redesign their breasts, hips, and faces through plastic surgery to achieve the masculine definition of what is sexy. They have let themselves become sex objects because what matters to them is not how they feel about themselves or even how they feel physically, but how the masculine culture sees them. The definition of what is sexy does not include the health, well-being, or subjective state of the dresser. Women who do dress more naturally, with flat shoes on their feet and clothes that cover their lower buttocks and navel, run the risk of being seen as undesirable.

Besides its effect on women's appearances, with the feminine in subjugation, compassion and nurturing seem to have been wiped from our collective souls. Does anyone know or care that our governmental agencies have institutionalized child abuse and neglect? At least 21 of our states have been under court supervision for failing to take proper care of children who have already been abused or neglected by their parents. According to news reports, judges across the country have found "outrageous deficiencies" in child-protection services. Child welfare officials are placing these children in unsafe or overcrowded foster homes and are not providing them with adequate medical care.[6] What kind of people are we that do not care about our children? Our most vulnerable children who cannot fend for themselves?

Women's Mental Health

Women's dislike of themselves because they have repressed the feminine is an underpinning for mental health problems such as depression, emotional and chemical dependency, eating disorders, and staying in abusive situations.

Would as many little girls be victims of sexual abuse if they valued their feminine selves and their female bodies? The same esteem little boys feel toward their masculine selves and their male bodies? Surely children with great self-esteem are better prepared to defend themselves.

Depression is an internal cry, a psyche pining for what is lacking and what is sorely needed for wholeness. Given our patriarchal beliefs, it should come as no surprise that one of every four women will suffer from a serious depression in her lifetime.[7]

Women, with a rate of depression at least double what it is for men,[8] are grieving for the feminine. The depression figures alone show that women have become too one-sided and too harsh in their condemnation of themselves. They lack the feminine principles of appreciation of their personal experience, compassion for the self, acceptance of feelings, connection to the unconscious, awareness of the physical body, and respect for human limitations. Women who find their feminine connection through depression often look back at this time as a blessing. During their struggle, their goal is simple. Overcome the depression. Stop the pain. Yet they discover post-depression that they have gained a greatly enhanced quality of life.

Dependent personality disorder is "a pervasive and excessive need to be taken care of that leads to submissive and clinging behavior and fears of separation."[9] The underlying cause is lack of strong personal identity. Each female child who isn't allowed to develop a feminine or a masculine identity is at risk for this disorder, as are all girls who are told by our culture that they are of limited or restricted value because of their gender. Full-blown personality disorders are rare, but what is quite common is for women to show dependency tendencies. A few years back, the chemical dependency movement defined co-dependency and turned it into a multi-million dollar industry. The resulting books, workshops, and support groups were stupendously popular because almost every woman, regardless of her circumstances, identified with the characteristics of dependency.

When too repressed and restricted, feminine energy may make itself known through compulsions such as chemical dependency and eating disorders. The next chapter goes into detail about how successful treatment for addictions seems to hinge on the feminine ways of surrendering, recognizing limitations, and forming genuine relationships with others. The destructive urges and feelings of the body overwhelm the addict, destroy her best intentions, humiliate her, and cause her to self-destruct over and over again—as if to show her over-inflated ego and highly prized intellect they are no match for (Terrible) Mother nature. Perhaps the meaning of addiction is that the hag has had enough. Her message to the addict is: "If you have no humility, you will experience humiliation."

it was a dream[10]

in which my greater self
rose up before me
accusing me of my life
with her extra finger
whirling in a gyre of rage
at what my days had come to.
what,
i pleaded with her, could i do,
oh what could i have done?
and she twisted her wild hair
and sparked her wild eyes
and screamed as long as
i could hear her
This. This. This.

Chapter Five

Valuing the Feminine

(My whole life was) devoted unreservedly to the service of my sex. The study and practice of medicine is, in my thought, but one means to a great end, for which my very soul yearns with intensest passionate emotion ... the true ennoblement of women, the full harmonious development of her unknown nature, and the consequent redemption of the whole human race.

Dr. Elizabeth Blackwell, 1871[1]

Remember Joseph Campbell's description of the feminine: "The dark, the moist, the receptive, passive, surrender, completion, modesty, relatedness, seduction, irrationality, fair enchantment." What do you think about these words as applied to the feminine? Applied to you?

We may feel disgraced or irritated by these words. Our reactions suggest we are not yet Sir Gawains who can totally embrace the feminine. Rather, we feel ashamed of her. Could we *really* find value in the feminine if we were to take a hard look? We are secretly afraid what we've been taught is right—that feminine characteristics imply inherent weakness, stupidity, or inferiority.

One way to think about the feminine (and the masculine) characteristics is the way the Taoists think of them. Yin and Yang are interdependent and complementary. Light exists only in contrast to darkness, moistness only in contrast to dryness, warmth only to cold. No characteristic could exist without its opposite. Active makes no sense without passive to act upon. Passive means nothing unless it is contrasted with activity. One aspect of a quality cannot exist—indeed has no value—without its opposite. The opposites are dependent on each other with each contributing equally to the whole.[2]

The Tao Te Ching says:

When people see some things as beautiful
other things become ugly....
Being and non-being create each other.
Difficult and easy support each other.
Long and short define each other.[3]

A second argument raises the possibility that what we have learned has been wrong in several ways. Our scientific paradigm judges masculine characteristics as superior to feminine characteristics. In other words, intellect is better than instinct, active is better than passive, logic is superior to passion. But Eastern philosophy tells us just the opposite, that the essence of life lies in the intuitive, the emotions, the mysterious.

Who is right—East or West? Many thoughtful people have concluded that both polarities are important to how we live our lives. Either approach, when one-sided, leads to dehumanizing conditions. In many Eastern countries, for instance, there is a deplorable standard of living because rationality and knowledge have not been valued along with logic, science, technology or self-determination. In the United States, there is depression, alienation, and violence because the "not rational"—intuition, instinct, wisdom—has not been valued or given expression; thus, we also ignore compassion, interdependence and mystery.

A third argument is a subset of the second. We view the feminine pejoratively because we have been conditioned to view feminine characteristics that way. If we were to take another earnest look, we might see the positive value of these characteristics. With masculine characteristics, our tendency has been the opposite—to focus on their positive aspects. We forget that masculine principles, taken to extreme, can be absurd, or, if used in the wrong circumstances, even harmful. We'll consider this argument more closely by studying several feminine characteristics.

Passive

"Passive" was one of the terms on the feminine list that initially gave me a queasy feeling. As a woman, I did not want to be identified with such a characteristic. Why? Because we equate passive with weakness and ineffectiveness; besides, we live in a society that values action and power. We believe there's nothing we can't do if we just work hard enough.

But those of us who are students of human behavior, as leaders, therapists, or teachers, have learned the importance of being passive. We have learned to wait to intervene, or not to intervene at all. We wait until the student is ready to do her work. We trust the process, trying not to interfere with it. We have learned that approaching certain situations with force or control can cause polarization and harmful outcomes. In fact, yielding to resistance can be our most effective tactic. For example, Gandhi and Martin Luther King, Jr. showed us how awesome passive nonresistance could be.

John Heider, a psychologist and interpreter of Taoism, writes of how one successfully leads psychotherapy groups:

Imagine that you are a midwife; you are assisting at someone else's birth. Do good without show or fuss. Facilitate what is happening rather than what you think ought to be happening. If you must take the lead, lead so that the mother is helped, yet still free and in charge.

When the baby is born, the mother will rightly say: 'We did it ourselves!'[4]

Surrender

"Surrender" is closely related to passive, but is possibly even more frightening to women who have felt powerless. Paradoxically, the reason Twelve Step programs (which to date have impacted many more men than women) have been extremely effective and popular is because they hinge on the process of surrendering. Surrendering is badly needed by masculine egos that have become too grandiose in their own separateness and unlimited power—for example, masculine egos that used alcohol, drugs, or food to escape the unconscious.

Literature from Alcoholics Anonymous has a good description of the individual who must surrender in order to overcome addiction:

> … far too smart for our own good. We loved to have people call us precocious. We used our education to blow ourselves up into prideful balloons, though we were careful to hide this from others. Secretly, we felt we could float above the rest of the folks on our brainpower alone. Scientific progress told us there was nothing man couldn't do. Knowledge was all-powerful. Intellect could conquer nature. Since we were brighter than most folks (so we thought), the spoils of victory would be ours for the thinking. The god of intellect displaced the God of our fathers.[5]

Step One says, "We admitted we were powerless over alcohol—that our lives had become unmanageable."[6] The alcoholic or the addict is in trouble because she has convinced herself that she is invincible. The laws that apply to ordinary humans do not apply to her. She has a touch of megalomania. Surrender and humility are necessary if she does not want to be sick and miserable. She must lay down the masculine attitude of "I can conquer anything" and accept the feminine attitude, which tells her she is limited. She cannot, does not and should not have power over certain substances, situations, and people.

Step Two states, "Came to believe that a power greater than ourselves could restore us to sanity."[7] Then, Step Three continues: "Made a decision to turn our will and our lives over to the care of God as we understood Him (sic)."[8] Twelve Step programs are not religious, but they are spiritual. To recognize a power beyond the human self, and to decide to have a relationship with such a power, requires a tremendous shift away from masculine consciousness and hubris. It calls for humility and surrender. St. Francis of Assisi said, "For it is in dying [to our ego selves] that we are born to everlasting life."

Each of the other nine steps continues this process of surrendering. Step Seven even uses the word "humbly." Step Ten says to promptly admit when one is wrong.[9] And one of the major tenets of Alcoholics Anonymous is to "Let go and let God."

Relationship

Before we move on from the Twelve Step programs, consider how useful another feminine attribute, "relationship," becomes for members of Twelve Step groups. Relationships with a higher power, relationships with the group, relationships with other recovering alcoholics or addicts, and relationships with those who need help are continually fostered and nurtured by the steps, the traditions, and the literature of the program.

Relationships are also crucial to the survival of this planet, especially our relationship with Mother Earth. Recently I read a news story that reveals our alienation from our Mother. My hometown of Austin, Texas, has been attempting to maintain an Oriental garden. Felix Warwas, the manager of the Taniguchi Oriental Garden, recounts how he has seen an increasing amount of broken statues, trampled flowerbeds and graffiti carved in the trunks of small trees. He didn't see such problems in Japan.

"What astonished me was how much the Japanese respect the garden. There's no paper on the ground, no trails cutting through. They don't even have to put up barricades. The garden is a living spirit to them."[10]

In an attempt to cut down on the damage in the garden, Mr. Warwas tries to accommodate the photographic needs of visitors by leaving a bed unplanted in front of a picturesque background, so they can walk there and pose for photos. But still, trampled flowers and crushed vines are all that remain where people have cut across beds. And both adults and children are doing the damage. He laments that American parents aren't teaching their children to treat gardens respectfully.

Irrationality

Women have also attempted to prove that they are not "irrational." We self-consciously guard against excessive emotional displays, illogical thinking and illogical speech. Yet, irrationality is beneficial, compelling and absolutely necessary. Consider a human who is only and totally rational, one for whom all decisions and behavior are based strictly on reason and logic. (I have met him, and he is boring and "nonhuman"!) Yes, the zest of life, the joy and spirit of life spring from imagination, feelings, intuitions—the unconscious—all irrational. Spontaneity, playfulness, love, and creativity are irrational functions without which no community could survive or would want to survive.

Many great scientific discoveries have broken through from the irrational—from dreams, hunches, accidents, or an idea that suddenly leaps into a scientist's mind. Without the irrational for inspiration, the rational would simply dry up.

As was shown earlier with the *Vierge Ouvrante*, our consciousness is influenced by our unconscious, whether or not we are aware of the link. Indeed, it is when we try to be rational thinkers with no psychic backgrounds that our troubles intensify. Extreme rationality leads to neurosis. One way or another, irrationality will be lived out.

The words we use to describe the feminine are humble attempts to capture the essence of an archetype. They can only be pieces of the truth, but at least they entice us to listen and ponder. Our culture has strained these words through its negative filter, attempting to strip them of all vitality and validity. We now have the capacity to remove the cultural filter, to discern the feminine wisdom contained in these words.

You can change the meaning of the feminine. Black is beautiful. Water is as powerful as fire. The feminine is ...

fine
> formidable

> feIsty

full, fuller, fullest, fullness, fulfilling

> FUNDAMENTAL

fabulous

> fairest of them all
> > fierce

facile

familiar Funky

frantic

frank f a n c i f u l

fervent

frivolous

fantastic

furious

festive

fascinating

ferocious

FUN FRIGHTENING friendly

fashionable

fortifying

favorable *fiery*

fruitful

fertile

functional

freeing

fortunate.

Chapter Six

The Valueless Woman

Considering the length of time that women have been dependent, is it surprising that some of them hug their chains, and fawn like the spaniel?

Mary Wollstonecraft, 1792[1]

A Story of an Abusive Relationship

I am sitting in my therapist chair listening to her recite the latest atrocities. Every week when she comes in, it's something. He was drunk again last night. He didn't pick their son up from baseball practice on Thursday as he had promised, and he stayed out all night. He humiliated her in front of their friends. He blackened her eye.

"Why doesn't she leave him?" I ask myself, and I am aware of my own frustration and anxiety because nothing has changed for her in the time she's been seeing me. She cries and says she knows she should get a divorce. She says her friends hate him; she can't trust him; they don't ever talk. Yet she continues in the relationship. She and I both feel her helplessness and defeat.

"Oh, from a practical standpoint," my mind muses, "she could leave." We've established this many times in our sessions. She has a good job, only one child to care for and supportive parents.

"But for the compulsion to be with this man." My thoughts have come full circle. The compulsion is so much stronger than the reasoning and logic and the "I know what I should do"— and stronger than me.

When I was working with this woman early in my career, I was puzzled about why she and women in similar situations stayed in abusive relationships. Sociological explanations (poor financial resources, no other place to live, too many children, inadequate education or training for a job) and the *battered spouse syndrome* were incomplete and unsatisfying answers. (The battered spouse syndrome theorizes that the wife gradually comes to believe she is no good, worthless, deserving of her beatings and is causing her partner to be out of control.)

"But how or why does the battered spouse syndrome occur in the first place?" I would wonder. Could it be that a woman who allows herself to be violated lacks her own sense of self? Perhaps she lacks a center, a self, from which to say no to a man to whom she is attached? With no basic sense of her own self-worth, she values the man and the relationship more than herself. In fact, she may have been overtly and covertly taught this very lesson: "Girls and women don't matter. Men and our ability to relate to them do." Valuing him more, she compromises herself— initially in subtle, perhaps inconsequential ways. Eventually this willingness, even eagerness, to compromise just to please him, sets in motion a relationship dynamic that results in violence and destruction.

Valueless Women as Girls

Some women believe they are nobody. They feel valueless. Because they have developed neither their masculine nor feminine core, their identity is taken from others. When they experience psychological pain or problematic situations, they have no reservoir of strength, no inner-contained self to direct them or to sustain them.

During childhood, especially girls who are raised in extreme patriarchal families, become who their family wants them to be. And, crucially, they learn from their father (and family) that they are not worthy of respect because they are females. They may be loved, even adored, but their father's love is similar to the love he has for a servant or a pet. As adults, these women tend to repeat the disappointment of this primary relationship over and over as they choose men who are not fully capable of loving and committing to them.

Girls in extreme patriarchal families are denied ground from which to develop a self. They are discouraged, even punished, if they should undertake such masculine propensities as showing initiative or analyzing situations. At the same time, they are shamed and devalued for any feminine attributes: They are told that crying is for sissies, enjoying music is a waste of time, and wanting to be pretty is vain.

The substantial activities are the ones the men and boys are engaged in, from which they are excluded. Rewards come from turning their attention and concentration to the care of their father and other people, as they see their mother doing. They become preoccupied with pleasing others because it's all they know and all they are rewarded for.

Dana's childhood prepared her to be a valueless woman. Dana's father was in the military, and he ruled his wife and girls as if they had also enlisted. His wife had accepted her subservient role in exchange for the security of being married long before Dana or her sisters were born. Mom was probably depressed during Dana's childhood. Dana certainly didn't remember any happy times with her. They all learned to "get out of the way" and be quiet when Dad was home. His grumpiness and demands were justified because he had been working hard all day "for them." Dana adored animals and begged for a pet, but she was never allowed to have one, as they were "too much trouble." She remembered loving to dance to music on the stereo as a small girl, but got the impression that this bothered her parents, so she stopped. Her inquisitiveness also went by the wayside for the same reason. If she expressed an emotion, she was told to quit being dramatic, and her father laughed at her when she said she'd like to be a doctor, telling her she wasn't smart enough to be anything but a housewife. When her little sisters misbehaved, she was blamed for not watching after them. Her weight gain during puberty was a source of anxiety for her parents. Initiative of any kind was discouraged by teasing. Dana and her sisters learned to make moderate grades in school, so as not to draw attention to themselves.

Valueless Women as Women

Valueless women typically latch onto a man or a series of men for their identity and self-worth.[2] Their magical, mystical male partners give them solutions and self-definition. Because they are usually involved in traditional female roles, our society mislabels these women as feminine. In so doing, society perpetuates the stereotype of feminine that many women fear.

Finding their identity through a man is accomplished by projecting what is valuable to him. Projection occurs when we experience our own qualities (of which we are unaware) as belonging to another. When we instantly dislike someone we meet, we are likely seeing in him or her some quirkiness of our own that we do not admit to ourselves. For example, I dislike and feel a little afraid when I am around forceful women because I am conflicted about being assertive.

Women who feel valueless perceive the positive qualities they cannot own as belonging to their partners. While the partner will have a smidgen of what she values—in fact, this bit of reality is the hook for the projection—often, he is mostly an illusion she has created and maintains.

Since it is culturally sanctioned for men to achieve, women often see their own hero possibilities as belonging to the man, working hard to foster his achievements. All the power in the relationship is given to the man. He chooses her. He decides if she is desirable. He determines their level of involvement.

When a woman believes her partner is wildly wonderful and she is woefully worthless, or even just mediocre, she is likely projecting. She is also probably listening to his words, but ignoring the behavior that does not match the projection.

Women who feel valueless believe their salvation will come from their relationship. But life offers no free rides. No prince will kiss Sleeping Beauty awake. The psychological work can only reside with each individual. A woman who experiences herself as valueless is not going to be in relationship with a psychologically mature person. Beyond her projections to him (and his projections to her), he feels as worthless as she does. Moreover, he plays this valuelessness out in his life to the same extent that she plays it out in hers. They are, after all, a matched set.

Women who don't have a good sense of self believe the solution to their psychological pain is to find the right man. But when they are psychologically immature, they attract psychologically immature men. When women have achieved their own level of psychological integrity, then, and only then, will they attract the man they want.

A woman who believes she is valueless derives her self-worth from the relationship itself, whereas her partner probably derives his self-esteem from other sources, such as his job, sports, hobbies, or from simply being male. Because the relationship is too crucial for her, she will do anything to ensure that it continues. Pleasing her partner becomes her highest concern. Her own moral principles, her physical and mental health, even relationships with family and children, can be compromised. After a while, she is conscious of herself only as a mirror of her partner's reaction. If the relationship is threatened in any way, she feels desperate because the identity she has created will perish if she doesn't have her partner. Then who will she be?

Co-dependency

A *co-dependent* woman, defined as someone who chronically sacrifices herself for others, is a woman who does not value herself.

Mary was 57 years old and suffering from depression and obesity when she became my client because her husband of 36 years had moved out and filed for divorce. She blamed herself for the divorce, just as she had blamed herself almost every time her husband had been angry or displeased during their marriage. She had made a career out of pleasing him. She thought she had found the way to have a lasting marriage: sacrifice her self and "Make him happy. Make him happy. Make him happy." But she hadn't counted on his selfishness and sense of entitlement, and his decision that what would make him happy was being single.

I doubted that Mary had ever had a sense of herself—what it would mean to authentically live her life—and so I told her that finding herself could be her compensation for losing her marriage, but she did not see this as much of a gift. For her, the pain of separation from her self-substitute, her husband, was unbearable. She was suicidal; after all she had lost what she had built her life around. In Mary's case, the death of the marriage was a double psychological death in that who she had made herself to be also died when her husband left.

What was this co-dependent marriage like? Mary worked and put her husband through college. She had no education or training beyond high school. She wanted to live in the city; he wanted to live in the country, so they moved way out into a rural area. They went to his family's home on holidays, to her family's when his family was out of town. She secretly thought he expected too much of their sons and was too hard on them. Sometimes she even thought he was verbally abusive to them, but she never tried to talk to him about it. He under-budgeted her on groceries, then complained she was spending too much money when she went over the limit he'd set, causing her great anxiety. He would seem to be angry with her about other things, but wouldn't tell her why. Neither of them ever really knew what the other was feeling, as feelings were assumed or guessed, but not discussed. Sex was on his terms, when he wanted it.

If we as parents can do anything for our daughters, let us foster in them a sense of self, the entitlement to live an authentic life, and pride in the feminine and in the masculine. Let us know that when our daughters marry, they will not end up being abused or co-dependent. Rather, we will have raised daughters who enter marriage as a whole person who is enhanced by the relationship.

Chapter Seven

The Animus-Possessed Woman

In feminism, there is a certain giving up of one's self. The choice was to be feminine or equal.

Sharon Stone, 1996[1]

Equal or Feminine?

The women's movement in the 60s and 70s and the feminism of the last several decades have encouraged women to develop their masculine side, and society now allows this growth as never before. Attempting to lead fuller lives, women and men have worked hard to throw off society's stereotypic feminine image.

They were sensible to disregard the feminine of the 1990s if *Cosmopolitan* magazine editor Helen Gurley Brown's definition was valid: "Even when we grow up, we are all girls. Girl is the feminine side."[2] Furthermore, all the Cosmo feminine-girl was supposed to care about was: "How big should the big O be?" and "How to hold a man by giving him his freedom."[3]

Sharon Stone probably reflects many women's beliefs with her quote at the beginning of this chapter. She fears she will have to give up being as smart, strong, and fast as her male friends if she is also feminine.

And what is this so-called third-wave feminism all about? Lawyers wearing stilettos and having a French manicure? Drew

Barrymore says "Charlie's Angels" is about the third-wave. The angels are "their feminine selves," and are also able to do "what men do in action films."[4] The third-wave definition of feminine is … sexy? For instance, *Cosmo Girl*, 2004, "476 Ways to Look Sexy for Spring."[5]

In 1992, Gloria Steinem wrote about self-esteem and the inner self, new territory for a woman who had been so instrumental in the outer women's revolution.[6] She had come to notice that she was not happy on the inside, even though she had so much success in the world. I believe that Ms. Steinem was searching for what was lost—the feminine—and discovered a more balanced way of being. Though she didn't put her concepts into the feminine-masculine framework, to me, her book was about integrating the feminine with the masculine.

Like Ms. Steinem, women living out the masculine principle are often "superwomen." They are successful mothers and wives. Many appreciate fine clothes and keep themselves physically fit. They are pursuing successful careers as teachers, administrative assistants, physicians, politicians, and CEOs.

Yet, in moments of quiet reflection and honesty, many women notice their own despair and uneasiness. In spite of their worldly success, their ability to do anything a man can do and more, something seems wrong. The "animus," which is the Jungian personification for the inner masculine side of woman, says, in typical animus fashion: "Ignore your feelings, work harder, accomplish more, and it'll be okay." And this animus voice is reinforced by people around us.

But Jungian psychologist Robert Johnson warns:

> If a woman remains firmly rooted in her femininity, she may make the most excellent use of masculine characteristics; but if masculine characteristics dominate

her basic personality, she will, at best, be only an imitation male.[7]

A soundless intuitive voice, hardly perceptible because of the animus' noise, responds to these women's dilemma by saying: "Follow the threads of desolation to the feminine." This voice cries that the unease women feel has its origin in their lack of authenticity to themselves. They are missing from their own lives when they have repressed the feminine.

The Animus

Just as the valueless woman has been tragically impacted by the patriarchy, the masculine-dominated woman has been pre-empted by the patriarchy. She has unwittingly identified with her enemy and become the patriarchy's ardent standard-bearer. Though she may achieve her goals, her exclusion and denial of the feminine leads her to feel despair, brittleness, and a lack of personal fulfillment.

Jungian psychologists describe her as "animus-possessed" when her inner masculine (the animus) is the dominant factor in her personality.[8] Think of the animus as the personification of an energy field or a complex that threads its way through a woman's psyche. This masculine counterpart is the sum total of all the woman's personal experiences with males and the masculine; also, he is an expression of the masculine archetype.

Since the animus is shaped by a woman's personal experience with the masculine, as well as by women's collective history with the masculine, the animus has the capacity to be both useful and detrimental.

Women who see themselves as victims are dominated by a negative animus that tells them they are weak, helpless, and not "as good as." Women who are successful in a "man's world," such as a corporation or academia, are helped by the positive animus who knows how to be objective, rational, and to accomplish and achieve. Most women benefit from some of the animus' positive attributes, but also suffer from some of his negatives.

All women are capable of developing their masculine side. To be sure, we should encourage our daughters to cultivate this side. A woman with a well-developed animus knows how to work hard and to persevere. She enjoys challenges and is ambitious for herself. She not only understands how to make it in male-dominated institutions, but she is also a positive role model for other women as she demonstrates that women can be intelligent, rational, active, assertive, and dedicated to goals and a career.

But when strengthening the animus brings damage to the feminine, women have traded one restriction for another. An animus-possessed woman does not accept herself. She limits her psychological potential by trying to be who she is not, rather than who she is.[9] Women who have integrated their feminine have a sense of completeness because their feminine selves, their feminine energy, is no longer repressed. It may only be in contrast to their new feelings of wholeness that they realize how split off or incomplete they had felt before.

Characteristics of the Animus

Almost all of us have probably experienced the animus as an inner tyrant—directing, controlling, criticizing and driving. The animus rushes to dominate when women are feeling vulnerable, confused, or weakened in some way. If you can identify critical thoughts with no mercy in your head, that is the animus: "Why'd you do that? Just wait 'til they find out. Can't you do anything right? You shouldn't have tried. You'll never be smart enough. Be careful; they'll think you're crazy."

An animus-possessed woman often develops her persona— her public self—at the expense of her authentic self. What matters to her is prestige, status, and how she looks to others. She shuts down her own feelings to please others when it suits her purpose. Most of all, the animus-possessed woman is emotionally cold. Because she has suppressed her own feelings she lacks empathy for others. She needs to win, to be in control and, in the process of getting her way, she is oblivious to others' feelings or esteem.

Women who did not receive the nurturance and protection they needed as children are candidates for animus possession. One solution for a girl living in a chaotic, unsafe home is to attach to a protective animus who is strong and forceful, even aggressive. When women are animus-possessed as adults, their primary emotion—anger—readily beefs up for a bout or to assert control whenever they might feel hurt, fearful, or vulnerable. The animus defends them from their greatest fear—that they will again be victimized. He defends them from feelings of vulnerability, hurt, or sadness—feelings that are unacceptable to them. Equally unacceptable and threatening for these women is to acknowledge their feminine selves, a part of them which is so intimately identified with their vulnerability.

We're more likely to find an animus-possessed woman (as well as the valueless woman) in the company of men then in the company of women. She believes men are more trustworthy and make superior leaders. She feels better about herself, more elevated in status, when she is communicating with a man rather then another woman.

The animus-possessed woman usually has a narration going on in her head about how she's doing; that is, she is constantly judged by her animus. She is overly sensitive to remarks or oversights from others because the animus is chewing her up inside with criticism. And, she treats others in the same way, showing herself to be judgmental, controlling, and hypercritical. Husbands, children, and employees feel they can do nothing right as far as she is concerned. But such a woman still feels inadequate, even when she is performing at an exceptional pace. The animus is a harsh taskmaster, demanding performance and perfectionism, when he is unchecked by the feminine.[10]

Animus Mothers

Ironically, many of us grew up with mothers who were animus-possessed, even though they lived out traditional female roles as housewives and mothers. With no value given to the feminine, it should not surprise us to remember the passive-aggressiveness our mothers used with us and with our fathers. The myth we all carry about moms who stayed at home in the "good old days" was that they were nurturing and warm. But in reality, Mom's controlling ways, unauthentic thoughts, criticisms, and overblown ambitions for her children may have been more prevalent then nurturing.

When I first started thinking about the feminine, I realized I had grown up in a family where there were women, of course, but just a shadow of the feminine. I had known the masculine of my father, uncles, and brother, and the animus possession of my mother, grandmother, and aunts. (And, sadly, I also learned the complementary attitude: women are valued less then men.)

Sue, a client, described a mother who put good meals on the table, took her to every Girl Scout meeting, made sure she was clean and wore the best clothes, and who almost never said "I love you," or had hugs for her kids. She seemed angry and preoccupied most of the time. She mothered out of duty, not joy, and her kids knew it.

Solutions to Animus Possession

The answer to animus possession is to strengthen the feminine. The animus can be a wonderful helper, a great source of power to a woman—when he is grounded in the feminine.

We live out the feminine more when we get in touch with what we are feeling. The feminine feels, while the animus thinks it best to repress feelings.

Recently I visited with a young woman, Kate, and her mother. As a young child Kate had been sexually abused by her stepbrother, and when she finally told her mother what was happening to her, her mother took action. But her mother's actions and decisions were based on a logical analysis of the situation. Kate's mom's lacked empathy for her daughter, and so she left her daughter's emotional well-being out of the equation. The mother bought Kate a lock for her bedroom door and watched her son like a hawk to be sure the abuse did not reoccur. And then, in the mother's mind, the abuse was over and done with.

Though she truly loved her daughter and wanted to protect her, she was oblivious to her feelings. She discounted her 10-year-old's attempt to communicate fear, confusion, anger and shame. The abuse was never discussed again. Kate was not taken to counseling. Instead she was left with a secret she was instructed not to tell, an ongoing fear of further abuse, and a belief that something was wrong with her because she couldn't do what her mother wanted and stop remembering and feeling.

Our feelings provide a counterbalance and grounding for our thoughts. Without them we are not compassionate. We are not humans, but machines. Kate's mother had so successfully suppressed her own feelings that she did not have the capacity to have empathy for her daughter: thus, she emotionally abandoned her with a gaping wound—just as she was entering pubescence.

If you notice that your interaction with another has a strident under-or overtone, break your animus possession by bringing awareness to the relationship. Move into the relationship by establishing emotional connection, or empathy, in the present moment. In the same manner, connect with yourself as if you were your own best friend when you are stressed or beating yourself up.

Being able to find compassion for yourself and others, versus judging yourself and others, is a feminine shift. Of course, you still take responsibility for your actions, but you understand that you are human and that you and others will make mistakes.

Switching from *analyzing* to *synthesizing* strengthens the feminine. The feminine likes to see the whole, not just the pieces or parts. Understanding and appreciating the truth in paradoxes is a synthesizing activity, and it usually brings a lightness to your view. You begin to recognize that there is not just one "right" or one "truth" which helps in solving disagreements or problems.

While masculine consciousness is goal-oriented, feminine consciousness is process-oriented. The masculine will drive to his destination, failing to notice or appreciate the journey, if the feminine is lacking. The animus tries to control others and situations for the sake of his goals, while the feminine knows to let go and accept when control is crazy or impossible. The feminine finds the means as important as the end: The way a child and her math teacher interact with each other, matters as much, maybe more, as the child learning her multiplication tables. Enjoying the present, enjoying learning, and giving the child a feeling of confidence, are examples of feminine contributions to the learning environment.

The animus is dominant in perfectionists who also miss the journey because only the destination matters. Lynch and Huang[11] suggest that when you notice the anxiety that comes with *perfection* (an outcome-oriented concept), you can replace it with *excellence* (a process-based concept). This refocuses attention inward on such pursuits as pride, self-esteem, courage, perseverance, satisfaction and fun in the execution of a well-thought-out plan, or a particular mechanical skill. Try gauging your self-worth by how you "play the game"—not by the results. Results, which can't be controlled anyway, are the by-products of a successful inner process, not the measure of your self-worth.

Being goal-driven often goes hand in hand with making cognitive demands. ("I must have a new black Acura in order to be happy," or "I demand she change her mind and go with me. If not, I will be miserable.") Too-much animus demands that people, places, and things conform to his expectations or desires. The animus tells you that you can't be happy unless you get exactly what you want. With help from the feminine, demands can be downgraded to preferences. ("It would be nice to have a new car, but I can be satisfied with this one another year," or "If she doesn't want to go with me, I can still attend the concert and have fun.") The feminine likes or prefers certain outcomes. She pitches in to work with the animus, but she knows her happiness does not have to depend on the end result.

Women have disappointing conversations when one of them is conversing from the animus. While a woman may be hoping to express her feelings and to be heard by her friend, the other woman, if animus-bound, will be rushing to solutions and advice. Why not help out your friend by gently saying, "I don't want advice. I want you to listen to me."

I still recall a conversation I had with an office worker one morning after I had been in a car accident on my way to work. Though I was not hurt, my car had made a 180-degree turn in the middle of the expressway and was badly damaged, and I was quite shaken. When I finally arrived at the office hours later, I began to nervously pour out my tale to her, but I only made it to the point of saying I hadn't seen the other car in my mirror before she emphatically stated, "Well, I always turn my head and look behind me before I change lanes." Her words jarred and shamed me; she was not recognizing my anxiety, but telling me what I should have done. I remember that I stopped talking and just walked into my office.

To the feminine, personal experience is a valid and valuable way of knowing and making sense of her world. Scientific fact, objective data, consensus opinions, and traditions are input that doesn't supersede her subjective knowledge about how she wants to live and what her truth is.

A counterbalance for too-much animus is to move our awareness of our physical selves out of our heads and into our bodies. Check yourself right now. Where is your awareness of yourself? If you are a typical Westerner, it is located outside or in your head. Move your attention into your chest or into your stomach. Can you not feel a subtle shift within yourself, and more of a sense of being connected with yourself? The animus resides in the head, the feminine in the body.

When I am aware of my animus possession, I have learned I can find a quiet place and evoke my feminine with music or poetry. Yoga and meditation also take away the "rightness" of the animus and create a more balanced feeling in my body, emotions, and mind.

Chapter Eight

Feminine Identity Development

*Women should perceive that the negative attitudes they hold
toward their own femaleness are the creation of an anti-feminist
society, just as the black shame at being black was the product
of racism.*

Shirley Chisholm, 1970[1]

Coming to terms with the feminine, the patriarchy, and the
relationship between the two may move you through various
stages of identity.[2] (See Table One.) As with all stage theories,
you may not experience all the stages or follow the same sequence,
and you may even recognize behaviors that would put you in
several stages simultaneously. See if you can understand where
you are in your feminine identity development from reading
and thinking about the stages.

The Masculine is Sovereign

Women in the first stage have conformed to the patriarchy.
They do not challenge assumptions about the feminine, having
automatically accepted the masculine and the patriarchal cultural
values. Lifestyles, value systems, and cultural/physical
characteristics esteemed by the masculine society are held high,
while most ideals that would suggest feminine or female are

Stages of Feminine Development Model	Attitude toward Self	Attitude toward Other Women/Feminine	Attitude toward Men/Masculine
Stage One - Conformity	Self-depreciating	Women/feminine depreciating	Men/masculine appreciating
Stage Two - Dissonance	Conflict between self-depreciating & appreciating	Conflict between women/feminine appreciating & depreciating	Conflict between men/masculine appreciating & depreciating
Stage Three - Resistance & Immersion	Self-appreciating	Women/feminine appreciating	Men/masculine depreciation
Stage Four - Introspection	Concern with basis of self-appreciation	Concern with nature of unequivocal appreciation	Concern with basis of men/masculine depreciation
Stage Five - Integrative Awareness	Self-appreciating	Women/feminine appreciating	Selective appreciation

Table One: Model of Feminine Identity Development

(Adapted from Donald R. Atkinson, George Morten, and Derald Wing Sue, *Counseling American Minorities*, 6th ed. Copyright © 2004, McGraw-Hill, New York, N.Y. By permission of the McGraw-Hill Companies.)[3]

viewed with disdain or repressed. Women in this stage spend an inordinate amount of time and energy on being physically attractive to men, and most believe they could be so happy if they could just make over their bodies to match the ideal. Their highest goals are to be attached to a man, or to be "as good as" a man, or both. They, perhaps unconsciously, demean themselves and other women for being women; thus, their self-esteem suffers. They do not question the patriarchal emphasis on achievement, rational thinking, intelligence, monetary success and power.

Most feminists are in this stage. Their desire is to live out the masculine and to get what the men have. The valueless woman and the animus-possessed woman also belong to this stage of identity development. Each in her own way conforms to the patriarchy. While the valueless woman has existed here for thousands of years, the presence of the animus woman is more recent.

But What About the Feminine?

When women begin doubting and questioning dominant beliefs, they move into a time of dissonance. New information or new experiences that are not consistent with patriarchal beliefs can be the catalysts, as well as no longer being rewarded for being in the conformity stage.

Sarah had never questioned her belief about men making better bosses. She assumed women were less objective, not as smart as men, and unable to lead others. But when she was moved into an organization where her female boss was readily accepted and admired, she began to doubt her old attitude.

The influx of Eastern religion and philosophy into our culture has challenged some Western values, as well as brought attention to the yin/feminine. (Chapter Nine will explore some of these criticisms of Western ideals and introduce some of the Eastern beliefs.)

Aging can strain some women's willingness to conform. When they begin to notice they are no longer appreciated for their appearance, they may face a personal crisis about their self-worth. And, if they decide to step out of the sex object role, they are, to some extent, freed from the conventions of society (because society has already rejected them).

Middle-class baby boomers are poised for dissonance. They have juggled family and jobs. They have had fabulous careers that were supposed to fulfill them. They've made their own money and had some measure of power. In other words, they have lived out the American (patriarchal) dream of success and happiness. But the women—and men—I know have found the dream wanting, and describe a strange stirring, a yearning for something more. This dissatisfaction is likely to intensify as they are now beginning to experience newfound freedom from the roles of sex object, reproduction, and motherhood. While they are the most empowered women we have ever known, they have not yet found the feminine. And the life they have not lived is calling to them.

Usually, movement into dissonance is gradual, but sometimes dramatic events propel women into disagreement. Women and men became aware of sexual harassment as they followed the Anita Hill/Clarence Thomas hearings. Some began to understand its relevance to their lives, sparking a national dialogue about how to define and reckon with it.

The whole country seemed to experience Hillary Rodham Clinton as a lightning rod for dissonance, which is why no one is neutral to the roles she has played. When her husband's sexual misconduct became public knowledge, one woman said to me, "Finally, Hillary is getting hers." Such animosity shows how threatening she is to the status quo.

Madonna has created discord. She has shoved our sexual double standard and our discomfort with women's sexuality in our faces. Dissonance has also been created when women discovered they could not make their own decisions about their bodies, about whether or not to continue a pregnancy even during the first trimester, and about whether or not to use certain contraceptives.

As women have a growing awareness of sexism, the next step is to confront their feminine identity. They now realize that not all aspects of the masculine are good—or good for them. They consider the possibilities of the feminine (and of women), and begin to develop a sense of pride in their feminine selves. Friendships with other women begin to blossom.

Except for Laura Secord[4] asks "But what about the feminine/women in our history?"

> This nation was founded by men,
> fought for   bled for
> divvied up by men who didn't
> eat dinner,
> change their underwear,
> make holes in their socks,
> or father children.
> We know this is true because
> women are not mentioned in
> history books, except for
> Laura Secord who invented
> ice cream with the help
> of her cow.
> Except for Laura Secord,
> women did not come from England
> and France, their footfalls
> did not stir the forests,
> their soup did not boil in
> fireplaces, their laundry
> never hung from trees,
> so their children remember
> them only in dreams.

Embracing the Feminine, Opposing the Masculine

In this stage, women's eyes have been opened, and they are profoundly aware of how they and the feminine have been oppressed. They are angry; they want it to stop. One way to bring an end to it while they are strengthening the feminine, is to reject the masculine and men.

Women in this stage can become absorbed in the discovery of their own history and culture; they actively seek out information and artifacts that enhance their sense of feminine identity and self-worth. The study and popularity of the ancient goddesses is an outgrowth of this desire to know the feminine, as well as women's art shows, women's music festivals, and even "chick flicks." Other supportive advances have been increased attention to women's health, women's new willingness to share experiences about their bodies and menopause, and the rise of women's history and women's studies as legitimate academic pursuits.

Feminine qualities that once elicited feelings of shame and disgust become symbols of pride. (Examples include choosing to be a stay-at-home-mom, instead of climbing the corporate ladder; emphasizing curves and some feminine fat, as opposed to a slender, boyish look; appreciating the talent, hard work, and perseverance that went into our grandmothers' needlework; admiring the quiet spirituality of women involved with the church.) A woman in this stage asks herself, "Why should I be ashamed of who and what I am? Why should I be ashamed of the feminine?"

Challenging cultural and personal attitudes defined the consciousness groups of the 70s, although they focused mostly on sex roles. Some women's groups today are more concerned with recognizing and appreciating the feminine, for instance the groups that have sprung up around *Women Who Run With the Wolves*. [5]

As women's self-esteem increases and they shape new identities, women feel more connected to other women as opposed to men. Women who have a true sense of self are now admired and respected, becoming the new role models.

While genuine friendships are developing among women, some may find their previous relationships with men threatening, unsatisfying, or angry. They either try to change the (oppressive) basis of these relationships, or leave the relationship altogether.

A number of women will deliberately restrict their interactions to other women as much as possible, and they will feel and direct considerable anger and hostility toward the patriarchy and men. For a while at least, male bashing could become a satisfying pastime. Though they may know better intellectually, they are not careful to distinguish between the attitudes and values of the patriarchy and the attitudes and values of individual men. Years of repressed anger spills out; in their eyes, all men are enemies. In its extreme form, women become revolutionaries, advocating for the destruction of all patriarchal institutions and structures. The famous bra-burners of the 1970s were such rebels, though there was a scarcity of the feminine in their actions. Today we find feminist separatist organizations that advocate having no contact with males. In many people's minds, these angry reactions and calls for separateness have come to define the feminist movement.

What About the Feminine and the Masculine Works for Me?

This stage, like the second one, is a time of questioning, re-evaluation, and introspection. When they have moved through their anger and are confident they will no longer allow oppression, women are ready to devote their energies to understanding themselves and incorporating aspects of the feminine and the masculine that work for them. They also begin to bear in mind the feminine values of integration and relationship that they may have laid aside.

But a woman attempting to move out of the previous stage may clash with friends who hold rigid views and who are unable to understand her desire for individuality. She may even experience pressure from them to end an enduring relationship with a man because "he" is the enemy.

The conflict for women can be between responsibility and allegiance to women as a group versus notions of personal independence and autonomy. Women realize men have also been oppressed by the patriarchy, and that some men are feminists. Moreover, they recognize and admire men who are engaged in the same process; who are striving to balance the feminine and the masculine within themselves. They also can see that many elements of the patriarchy are highly functional and desirable, and they seek to incorporate these elements into their lives without losing the feminine once again.

Marriage of the Feminine and the Masculine

The last stage is one of balance and integration. Having developed respect for the feminine, and thus an inner sense of confidence, women can now also own and appreciate beneficial aspects of the masculine. They recognize that some men can be trusted and liked, and they can be open to the constructive aspects of the masculine culture, while working to change its destructive features. Most important of all, they like themselves as women. They are rooted in the feminine, and they appreciate the masculine side of themselves. They are our leaders for psychological wholeness.

Chapter Nine

The Feminine in Religion

When God set the heavens in place, I was present.
I was by God's side, a master craftswoman.

Sophia, 8000 B.C.[1]

Marion Zimmer Bradley in *The Mists of Avalon* portrays the early conflict between the religion of the Goddess and the Christian religion. The Christianity of A.D. 500, dominated by the patriarchy, would not tolerate the concept of the deity as both feminine and masculine. The Goddess religion, on the other hand, accepted different forms of worship because it believed everyone was ultimately worshiping the same deity:

> For all the Gods are one God … and all the Goddesses are one Goddess, and there is only one Initiator. And to every man his own truth, and the God within.[2]

As the story goes, the Christian priests insisted on destroying the Goddess religion.[3] Although Zimmer Bradley's story is fictional, it is based on historical evidence that the Yahweh of the Old Testament was a jealous god, and that his followers were threatened by and did set out to destroy the older Goddess-based religions. Indeed, historical scholars point to veiled references to the Goddess religions in the Old Testament and to warnings by Yahweh and his prophets of its evil nature.[4]

Christianity

We still see the vestiges of this attitude in Christianity today. (Judaism and Islam, coming from the same desert region and sharing the same teachings of the Old Testament as Christianity, are also religions based in the masculine.) Mainstream and evangelical Christian churches teach their members, the majority of whom are women, to worship a father and a son. Catholics relate to Mary as an intermediary, a holy one who is almost goddess-like but, nonetheless, still not totally divine like the father and the son.

The Symbol of God Functions[5]

The church's portrayal of God as male has profound implications for women's view of themselves. When the son and the father are worshiped, women and girls are marginalized. [6] They are not like their God. They can never be like him. The subtle, pervasive underlying meaning is that the feminine has little value and that females can never be good enough.

Recently the Southern Baptists, the largest Protestant denomination in the United States, complained so voraciously about a gender-neutral translation of the Bible in progress that it was killed. Conservative Southern Baptists objected to what they said was "capitulation to feminism and political correctness."[7] A professor at a Baptist theological seminary was quoted: "It's a victory for the word of God. You don't compromise Scripture just to make women feel included."[8]

Perhaps some in the church would protest that "God the Father" is not to be taken literally, but as a metaphor or personification for the nature of the divine. Still, the masculine god as metaphor or personification proves the point about what is highly valued in religion. As metaphor, it is intractable to some. Why has it been narrowed to exclude the feminine? Why would it seem like a sacrilege to use a metaphor that is inclusive?

In denominations that "allow" women ministers, much is business as usual. Female ministers, assimilated into the patriarchy, preach from the Bible without apology for its sexism. Fundamentalist churches preach the doctrine of family values, which is code for the man is the head of the family while the virtuous woman knows her place. Men hold the majority of the top leadership positions in any church's hierarchy—the positions with real influence and power.

The prayer recited every Sunday in most Christian churches is the *Our Father*. If you open a hymnal from almost any denomination you will find that little attempt has been made to eliminate sexist language. A quick glance at a hymnal reveals words such as "king," "brotherhood," "men," and, even "sonlight."[9]

Elizabeth Johnson tells us of church language:

... the daily language of preaching, worship, catechesis, and instruction conveys ... : God is male, or at least more like a man than a woman, or at least more fittingly addressed as male than as female. The symbol of God functions.... Wittingly or not, it undermines women's human dignity as equally created in the image of God.[10]

Transcendence and Immanence

Most Western religions emphasize the transcendent aspect of God, as opposed to God's immanent nature. Transcendence and immanence are the Yin and Yang, or the feminine and masculine nature of God. God, the transcendent, is the divine as separate and apart from humans. He is God the Father, and he has great and terrible power. He lives in Heaven, or is thought of as spirit apart from humans. He is prayed to, and he may or may not intervene in human affairs. The Yin of God, the immanent, is more the focus of Eastern religion. The immanent is the immediate presence of God, closer than breath, nearer than hands: God and God's creation existing within each other. The immanent God is our Mother, most merciful. She is everywhere we are—in nature, in the Earth, in our hearts. As such, she is reminiscent of the *Vierge Ouvrante Open*, the statue of the eternal feminine, enfolding the father and the son.

Sexism is Sinful[11]

If the purpose of religion is to draw us to spirit, most Western religions are betraying women and men. Elizabeth Johnson strikes a chord when she says that a religious symbol or custom which results in the denigration of (the feminine and) women can not be spiritually true.[12] "Sexism is sinful ... it is a ... breaking of the basic commandment—'Thou shalt love thy neighbor as thyself.'"[13]

Sophia

Feminist theologians write about Sophia—a thinly disguised feminine figure found in the Bible. In an attempt to depersonalize and to de-gender her, the writers of the Old Testament referred to her as "Wisdom." Sophia, the name for wisdom in the Greek language, occupies the first nine chapters of Proverbs. She is also prominent in the books that are contained in the Catholic Bible, but that are excluded from the Protestant Bible.[14]

Sophia is a female goddess-like figure who probably came out of the tradition of Jewish Wisdom theology from about the third century B.C. Over time, the patriarchy and the male scribes were successful in repressing her, not only from theological documents, but from the minds of the people.[15] Sophia originally symbolized the divine feminine, then she was downgraded to the partner of the male God. Finally, she was successfully repressed altogether. Perhaps while Sophia originally stood for wisdom, Yahweh originally stood for knowledge. Some theologians speculate that her attributes were given to Jesus.[16] The figure of the *Vierge Ouvrante, Open,* is reminiscent of Sophia.

Sophia speaks for herself in Proverbs 8:27-31:

When God set the heavens in place, I was present ...
I was by God's side, a master craftswoman,
Delighting God day after day,
ever at play by God's side,
at play everywhere in God's domain,
delighting to be with the children of humanity.[17]

Have you ever heard a minister, woman or man, read or interpret this Bible passage from the pulpit?

Christian Mysticism

Matthew Fox, a defrocked Catholic priest, is a Christian mystic and author who found his way of worshiping incompatible with established Western religion. Mysticism is feminine, he tells us, and he finds our societal denial of mysticism evident in the way we treat Mother Earth and in the way we treat the feminine principle as a negative force in our lives. The meaning of mysticism is a direct and personal experience of the divine. Mysticism is the experience of non-separation, or non-dualism, between God and humans. Mystics experience compassion, an inner knowing, and affirmation of all in the world.[18]

Matthew Fox offers "A Litany of Deliverance":

From Patriarchy's dualism,
From Patriarchy's violence,
From Patriarchy's lack of imagination,
… From Patriarchy's separation of head from body,
From Patriarchy's preoccupation with sex,
From Patriarchy's fear of intimacy,
From Patriarchy's crucifixion of Mother Earth,
… From Patriarchy's matricide, spare us O Divine One.[19]

Gnosticism

Gnosticism can be contrasted with orthodox Christianity as a religion based in the feminine. Gnosticism is a mystical branch of Christianity that lost out to the official teachings of the New Testament. Its followers were devoted first-century Christians. They were called *gnostic* because they derived their knowledge from their own "secret way," from their own observations and experiences, and not from authority.[20]

Gnostics point to the immanence of God. Rather than a God who is wholly other and separate, they believe the divine and the self are one. In the Gnostic texts, Jesus is an enlightened guide, instead of the one and only Son of God. His teachings focus on illusion and enlightenment, not on sin and repentance.[21]

The Gnostic attitude toward women and the feminine is inclusive and affirming. God is "God the Father" and "God the Mother" and is described with masculine and feminine elements. One author describes God as a dyad, one half of which is "the Ineffable, the Depth, the Primal Father"; the other half, he describes as "Grace, Silence, the Womb and 'Mother of the All.'"[22] Evidence even points to women who are considered equal to men in some of the gnostic groups, and many of the leaders in the Gnostic texts are women.[23]

A creation poem from the Gnostic text is spoken in the voice of a feminine divine power. It evokes echoes of Sophia and of the Vierge Ouvrante:

> For I am the first and the last.
> I am the honored one and the scorned one.
> I am the whore and the holy one.
> I am the wife and the virgin ...
> I am the barren one,
> I am the silence that is incomprehensible ...
> I am the utterance of my name.[24]

Taoism

Like Gnosticism, *Taoism*—an ancient philosophy and religion of China—is one of the few religions that gives prominence to the feminine. Mythically and historically, Taoism counts many women among its great figures.[25] It has been contrasted to Confucianism, the other Chinese religion and philosophy that is based in the masculine. Whereas Confucianism is a litany of rules and standards for living, Taoism is opposed to ideology. It is mystical, enigmatic, intuitive, and stresses the superiority of right action. Right action is learning to go with the flow of the universe, yielding, becoming a part of the whole. When one is aware and aligned with the forces of nature (Tao), Taoism teaches that a remarkable power (Te) will emerge. Bad action, which leads to disastrous consequences, is using force and power to make events happen.[26]

Lao Tzu, in Chapter Six of the *Tao Te Ching*, says:

The mystery of the valley is immortal;
It is known as the Subtle Female.
The gateway of the Subtle Female
Is the source of Heaven and Earth.
Everlasting, endless, it appears to exist.
Its usefulness comes with no effort.[27]

Sri Ramakrishna

To many Hindus, Sri Ramakrishna, who lived in the mid-1800s, was the living embodiment of the Divine. The Hindus view him as many Christians would view Jesus. Sri Ramakrishna was brought to enlightenment by his devotion to Kali, the Divine Mother.

A few months after his wife joined him at his temple, Sri Ramakrishna arranged a special worship of Kali, the Divine Mother. But instead of the image of Kali, he placed his wife, Sarada Devi, on the seat of worship. The worshiper and the worshiped went into a deep meditative state. After several hours Sri Ramakrishna came down again to the relative plane, sang a hymn to the Great Goddess, and surrendered himself before the living image of Kali, his wife. This is known as a Tantra ritual, the "Adoration of Woman." It is said that Sri Ramakrishna realized the significance of the great statement of the (Hindu document) Upanishad:

O Lord, Thou art the woman, Thou art the man; Thou art the boy, Thou art the girl; Thou art the old, tottering on their crutches. Thou pervadest the universe in its multiple forms.[28]

American Indians

The Sioux's traditional societies are matriarchal, with a religion based in the feminine. Russell Means, a Sioux writing about his religion, says: "When you understand matriarchal societies, you can understand life itself because women create. Women create and give birth. My God, they give birth."[29]

And, "They're the only living beings on Earth purified naturally by the universe, in exact time with the moon. How can God be a male entity? I find that insulting."[30]

He further argues that all man-made religions justify imperialism and male supremacy.[31]

Spirituality is Life

Spirituality is a calling to life. Life is a calling to spirituality. Is your religion giving you life, or injury and oppression? Does it enhance you as a human and spiritual being? Is it making your life more excellent, more beautiful, more loving? The religions developed and promoted by the patriarchy perpetuate low self-esteem in women by:

- presenting an image of God that is exclusively masculine (and male) as in the "father, son, and the (asexual) holy ghost";
- teaching masculine principles and ignoring feminine principles;
- teaching from sexist doctrine, such as the Bible;
- ignoring the contributions of the feminine to creation, relationships, the family, creativity, and the physical and psychological life processes (For example, where are the religious rituals celebrating the birthing powers of women?);
- doing nothing to dispel the myth of women as evil or, at best, as inferior to men;

- remaining silent about violence against women (A United Nations report concluded that "… violence against women is a function of the belief, … that men are superior and that the women they live with are their possessions or chattel they can treat as they wish.");[32]
- failing to minister to the special needs of women; even cultivating and reinforcing the helplessness of our mothers in the older generation;[33]
- providing limited information about women as spiritual leaders, historically or currently;
- filling the better jobs such as senior pastor and executive administrative positions almost exclusively with males;[34]
- denying women ordination as priests or ministers in some denominations;
- excluding women, women's experiences, and the feminine from their doctrine;
- failing to include the feminine in their language.

Victor White observes:

Where the god is male and father only, and … is associated with law, order, civilization, … religion … tends to … neglect … nature, instinct, … feeling, eros, … Such a religion, so far from 'binding together' and integrating, may all too easily become an instrument of repression, and so of individual and social disintegration.[35]

Mary and Martha[36]

On Sundays, the preacher said ladies were not
to speak in church. I watched light stream through Mary
in the stained glass window, through her uplifted
face, conversing with the best mind of the age.

Behind her, Martha, tiny shadow figure
in the pane, between lead, holding a heavy
tray, blocking light with her dark dress. Jesus said
Mary had chosen the better part. I knew.

But how to answer Mother—years of Martha
work for her and children's pain in the dark night—
when she said to me, "Girl, this, too, will be yours."

Chapter Ten

The Conscious Feminine

She who knows the [male], yet cleaves to what is [female]
Becomes like a raven, receiving all things under heaven.
                                    Lao Tzu, 6th Century B.C.[1]

Changing Our Beliefs

I first met black people when, as a child, I moved with my family to the Mississippi Delta in the 1950s. What I soon learned was that they "knew their place." They hung their head, wouldn't look a white person in the eye, and seemed eager to do whatever a white person asked of them, even a young girl like me. I felt uncomfortable around them because, whether they did believe they were inferior to whites or not, they surely did act as if they believed it.

Then along came the civil rights movement, and I began to see a scattering of blacks here and there who showed by their speech and their behavior that they were different. They felt pride in themselves, perhaps even believing they were equal to any other human being. Eventually, someone coined the phrase "Black is beautiful," and the truth of the idea seemed to explode in the minds of both black and white people. Some whites turned to violence in a desperate attempt to hold onto a way of life that was dying, but they knew they had already lost. The basic truth that "all men (sic) are created equal" was reverberating throughout the South.

The genius and the miracle of the civil rights movement was the ability to take what had been denigrated by the dominant culture and to turn it on its face. The ability to comprehend the falseness of how black people had been viewed, and how they had viewed themselves. The ability to change the very definition of what it meant to be black.

Are we now ready to do the same for the feminine archetype and for women? Women of certain classes and in certain areas of the world have literally been enslaved from the third century B.C. until this century. Oppression of women has existed for about 40 centuries.[2] During the 14th century and through the King Arthur legend of Gawain, the idea of sovereignty for women was expressed; yet it has taken six centuries more to achieve actual legal sovereignty for women, and then in only a smattering of countries. Could it be, after 4,000 years of the patriarchy, we are now ready for a change in human consciousness that would give the feminine her rightful place?

The New Feminine

A universal symbol of the historical feminine has been mother, whether in her good or negative aspects. Black women in our culture have inspired the new symbol—sister. A sister is someone who can stand alone and claims her power as a friend, an equal, and a contemporary. She implies a horizontal relationship with others, rather than the vertical relationships of mother and child or wife and husband. She is a virgin in the original sense of the word, meaning she is independent of man. She is contained within herself; her identity is her own because it is rooted in her feminine. She is in relationship with everything: the world, the environment, herself, her work, her society, individuals, people in need of her care, people whose care she needs. Moreover, because her relationships are full and reciprocal, her identity comes from them all and from none of them.

A sister listens to herself to determine her right action, and she shows the way for others. She takes her life seriously, knowing it is meaningful to the universe. She is reflective, self-correcting, authentic; she experiences the full range of human emotions, delighting in being female.

Organizations devoted to sisterhood, both formal and informal, strengthen women's self-concepts. From the various orders of nuns in the Catholic Church, to women's therapy groups, to informal Tuesday morning get-togethers over coffee, women have a feeling of being involved in something almost subversive when sisterhood is emphasized. This is because their exclusive gathering acknowledges value in something not masculine. "Sister" implies realization of the feminine. A feminine that is known, valued, and lived. A feminine who is full unto herself.

Demeter and Persephone

The myth of Demeter and Persephone shines through the ages to offer us the possibility of this new feminine. The Greek goddess Demeter was the "bringer of the seasons and of splendid gifts".[3] She was goddess of grain and of the harvest; her duties included supplying earthly humans with sustenance.

She and her beautiful daughter, Persephone, lived an idyllic life, but it was not to last. Zeus, the highest of the male gods, conspired with his brother, Hades, the god of the underworld, to kidnap Persephone so Hades could have her for his bride.[4]

Persephone was "the most beautiful among the flowers of the field ... her hair smells of praise. She is covered with butterfly wings as they hatch." And Hades wants "... the most beautiful flower of the field ..." As Persephone plucked flowers "... a column of horses gushed from the ground ..." Their rider, Hades, "His own eyes black among the marigolds, hands black, among the poppies, arms black with the soot of untold cremations among anemones ..." And Persephone "... recognized the bridegroom to whom she had been condemned though she did not want him ..."[5]

Demeter heard Persephone's screams; she searched everywhere, but her daughter was gone. After many days Demeter learned the horrible truth: "a pain more awful and savage reached Demeter's soul."[6] Her daughter, now in the underworld, had been forced to be the wife of Hades.

Demeter pleaded with various (male) gods to intercede with Zeus, but they and Zeus ignored her. When she could see no hope for Persephone's return, she "kept on wasting with longing for her ... daughter."[7] Then, the Homeric hymn tells us she brought a dreadful year:

> ... no seed in the earth sprouted. ...
> In vain the oxen drew many curved plows over the fields,
> and in vain did much white barley fall into the ground.
> And she would have destroyed the whole race of mortal
> men with painful famine ...[8]

Now Zeus, finally seeing that Demeter would destroy the earth, ordered Hades to bring Persephone back to her mother. But, because Persephone had eaten a seed Hades offered her from the pomegranate, she would have to return to Hades during winter. Mother and daughter, the gods, and the humans celebrated Persephone's return. Demeter fertilized the earth and it burst forth with fruit, grain, and corn.[9]

As a mother and a daughter, and with empathy for my own daughter, I relate to the sorrow, destruction, outrage, hope, and transformation portrayed by this myth. It also expresses the universal and timeless theme of women losing their innocence and suffering greatly because of life circumstances.

As a story of the feminine archetype, it tells of the time when the feminine value was destroyed and of the consequences of that devastation. The beloved, the promise of the future, the new feminine, is torn away from her mother, the older order of feminine nature (the collective unconscious). She is overpowered, raped, and changed forever. The feminine is sent to Hell. She is sent to the void of darkness and disgrace. If the gods have their way, she will be lost forever.

But the mother will not rest. She will not accept her separation from her daughter. She roams the world, sorrowing, searching for her. She bargains with the gods for her release. Ultimately, she causes famine; the land is barren and living creatures are starving. Consciousness is sterile; legalism crushes creativity; the earth and human nature are neglected; egoism runs rampant; over-intellectualism replaces reflection. As people begin to suffer and die, the gods eventually understand what life is like when the feminine is buried and inaccessible. Finally, they strike a bargain for Persephone's return.

Glory! What a difference the feminine's presence makes to the earth. Springtime blooms. Flowers and fruits and grains and grasses are resplendent. People laugh and play and love each other. Baby lambs and human babies are born and welcomed and loved. Masculine rape and abduction have been overcome. Our sister, the new feminine, has been transformed and redeemed by her experience in the underworld and by the masculine gods' recognition of her. Her return renews nature and human life.

Persephone's eating of the pomegranate seed and subsequent need to return to Hades for a portion of each year signifies the new interdependence and synthesis of the masculine and the feminine. Consciousness is informed by unconsciousness; unconsciousness co-creates with consciousness. Light is in darkness; darkness is in light. The masculine and feminine respect each other and each is given their rightful place.

The myth ends with the daughter and mother joyously reuniting as an expression of the completion of the feminine.

The completed feminine, the honored feminine, the living feminine: Are we ready? We are both of them, Demeter and Persephone, longing for recognition, appreciation, and fulfillment. Our melancholia is our desire to reunite with our primordial feminine selves. Our restlessness is our search for our daughter: the replenishing eternal feminine. May we each do what we must to make this union happen.

> *Beauty is life when life unveils her holy face.*
> *But you are life and you are the veil.*
> *Beauty is eternity gazing at itself in a mirror.*
> *But you are eternity and you are the mirror.*[10]

NOTES

Dedication

1. Bradley, Marion Zimmer. *The Mists of Avalon.* New York: Ballantine Books, 1982, p. 875.

Introduction

1. Gibran, Kahlil. *The Prophet.* New York: Alfred A Knopf, 1963, p. 76.

2. Neumann, Erich. *The Great Mother.* Princeton: Princeton University Press, 1963, p. 330-331.

3. Gibran, Kahlil. *The Prophet.* New York: Alfred A Knopf, 1963, p. 76.

Chapter One

1. Jung, C.G. *Psychology and Alchemy. Collected Works,* Vol. 12. Princeton: Princeton University Press, 1968, p. 208.

2. Johnson, Elizabeth A. *She Who Is: The Mystery of God in Feminist Theological Discourse.* New York: Crossroad, 1997.

3. Neumann, Erich. *The Great Mother.* Princeton: Princeton University Press, 1963, p. 330-331.

4. *Revised Standard Version of the Bible.* New York: Thomas Nelson and Sons, 1952. Isaiah 11:6.

5. *Revised Standard Version of the Bible.* New York: Thomas Nelson and Sons, 1952. Gen. 3:16.

6. Walker, Barbara G. *The Woman's Encyclopedia of Myths and Secrets.* San Francisco: Harper and Row, 1983, p. 290.

7. Lerner, Gerda. *The Creation of Patriarchy.* New York: Oxford Press, 1986.

8. Starhawk. *Spiral Dance.* San Francisco: Harper, 1989.

9. Bolen, Jean Shinoda. *Crossing to Avalon.* San Francisco: Harper, 1994.

10. Shore, Lesley Irene. *Healing the Feminine.* St. Paul: Llewellyn, 1995.

11. Easwaran, Eknath. *The Bhagavad Gita for Daily Living, Volume 1: The End of Sorrow.* Petaluma, CA: Nilgiri Press, 1975, p. 105.

Chapter Two

1. Rich, Adrienne. "Turning the Wheel," *A Wild Patience Has Taken Me This Far: Poems 1978-1981.* New York: W.W. Norton & Co., 1981.

2. Jung, C.G. *The Archetypes and the Collective Unconscious. Collected Works,* Vol. 9,1. Princeton: Princeton University Press, 1980.

3. Sanford, John A. *The Invisible Partners.* New York: Paulist Press, 1980, p. 8.

4. Adapted from Sanford, John A. *The Invisible Partners.* New York: Paulist Press, 1980; and from Singer, June. *Androgyny.* Garden City, New York: Anchor Books, 1977.

5. Sanford, John A. *The Invisible Partners.* New York: Paulist Press, 1980, p. 8.

6. Adapted from Sanford, John A. *The Invisible Partners.* New York: Paulist Press, 1980; and from Singer, June. *Androgyny.* Garden City, New York: Anchor Books, 1977.

7. Campbell, Joseph. *Masks of God: Creative Mythology.* New York: Penguin Putnam, 1976.

8. *The Random House Dictionary of the English Language.* New York: Random House, 1983.

9. Neumann, Erich. *The Origins and History of Consciousness.* Princeton: Princeton University Press, 1973.

10. *Ibid.*

11. Eisler, Riane. *The Chalice and the Blade.* San Francisco: Harper, 1988.

12. Neumann, Erich. *The Origins and History of Consciousness.* Princeton: Princeton University Press, 1973.

13. *Ibid.*

14. *Ibid.*

15. *Ibid.*

16. Perera, Sylvia. *Descent to the Goddess: A Way of Initiation for Women.* Toronto: Inner City Books, 1981, p. 16.

17. *Ibid.,* p. 17.

18. *Ibid.,* p. 17.

19. Wolkstein, Diane. *Inanna* (video). Montvale, N.J.: Cloudstone, 1988.

20. *Webster's New World College Dictionary,* Third Edition. New York, New York: Simon and Schuster, *1997.*

21. Neumann, Erich. *The Origins and History of Consciousness.* Princeton: Princeton University Press, 1973.

Chapter Three

1. King, John. "Professor Gingrich gives class synopsis of gender differences." New York Times Service. *Austin American Statesman,* January *19, 1995.*

2. Barton, Clara. *History of Women Suffrage, V,* 1922. In Carol McPhee and Ann Fitzgerald, *Feminist Quotations: Voices of Rebels, Reformers, and Visionaries.* New York: Thomas Y. Crowell, 1979.

3. Lerner, Gerda. *The Creation of Patriarchy.* New York: Oxford Press, 1986.

4. "Lawyer honored for equal rights." Associated Press. *Austin American Statesman*, August 7, 1995.

5. Lerner, Gerda. *The Creation of Patriarchy.* New York: Oxford Press, 1986.

6. "Peru could end law that frees rapists." Associated Press. *Austin American Statesman*, March 13, 1997.

7. Jordan, Mary. "Crime without punishment." The Washington Post. *Austin American Statesman*, July 13, 2002.

8. Crow, Karen. "For women, good old days weren't." Miami Herald. *Austin American Statesman*, December 16, 1993.

9. Lerner, Gerda. *The Creation of Patriarchy.* New York: Oxford Press, 1986.

10. Jung, C.G. *Analytical Psychology: Its Theory and Practice: The Tavistock Lectures.* London and New York, p. 183. *Collected Works*, Vol. 18. Princeton: Princeton University Press, 1980.

11. Jung, C.G. *Memories, Dreams, Reflections.* New York: Vintage Books, 1965.

12. "Roosevelt 'Great' in Jung's Analysis." *New York Times*, October 4, 1936.

13. Neumann, Erich. *The Great Mother.* Princeton: Princeton University Press, 1963.

14. Jung, C.G. *Psychology and Religion: West and East. Collective Works*, Vol. 11. Princeton: Princeton University Press, 1980, paragraph 391.

15. Neumann, Erich. *The Origins and History of Consciousness.* Princeton: Princeton University Press, 1973, p. 210-211.

16. Neumann, Erich. *The Great Mother.* Princeton: Princeton University Press, 1963, p. 233.

17. Neumann, Erich. *The Great Mother.* Princeton: Princeton University Press, 1963, p. 233 - 234.

18. Neumann, Erich. *The Great Mother.* Princeton: Princeton University Press, 1963.

19. *Ibid.*

20. Jung, C.G. *Psychological Types. Collected Works*, Vol. 6. Princeton: Princeton University Press, 1970, p. 135.

Chapter Four

1. Compiled from Johnson, Robert A. *Femininity Lost and Regained.* New York: Harper & Row, 1990. And Murdock, Maureen. *The Heroine's Journey.* Boston: Shambhala, 1990.

2. *Ibid.*

3. Jung, C.G. *The Psychology of the Child Archetype. Collective Works,* Vol. 9. Princeton: Princeton University Press, 1959/1968.

4. Peiken, Matt. "Girls' self-images take disturbing turn." St. Paul Pioneer Press. *Austin American Statesman,* October 10, 1997.

5. Reilly, Patricia Lynn. *A God Who Looks Like Me: Discovering a Woman-Affirming Spirituality.* New York: Ballantine Books, 1995, p. 214.

6. Pear, Robert. "Many states ignore orders to protect abused children." The New York Times. *Austin American Statesman,* March 17, 1996.

7. McGrath, Ellen. *When Feeling Bad is Good.* New York: Bantam Books, 1992.

8. Pajer, Kathleen. "New strategies in the treatment of depression in women." *Journal of Clinical Psychiatry,* 56(2), 30-37, 1995.

9. American Psychiatric Association. *APA Diagnostic and Statistical Manual of Mental Disorders,* 4th Ed. DSM-IV. Washington, D.C.: American Psychiatric Association, 1994, p. 665.

10. Clifton, Lucille. "it was a dream," *The Book of Light.* Port Townsend, WA: Copper Canyon Press, 1993.

Chapter Five

1. Beilenson, Evelyn and Tenenbaum, Ann (Ed.). *Wit and Wisdom of Famous American Women.* White Plains, N.Y.: Peter Pauper Press, Inc., 1995.

2. I first read this idea in Singer, June. *Androgyny.* Garden City, N.Y.: Anchor Books, 1973.

3. Mitchell, Stephen. *Tao Te Ching.* New York: Harper Perennial, 1988.

4. Heider, John. *The Tao of Leadership.* New York: Bantum, 1986, p. 33.

5. Alcoholics Anonymous World Services, Inc. *Twelve and Twelve.* New York: Alcoholics Anonymous World Services, Inc., 1952, p. 29.

6. *Ibid.,* p. 21.

7. *Ibid.,* p. 25.

8. *Ibid.,* p. 34.

9. Alcoholics Anonymous World Services, Inc. *Twelve and Twelve.* New York: Alcoholics Anonymous World Services, Inc., 1952.

10. Claitor, Diana. "Master Planters." *Austin American Statesman,* October 19, 1997, p. E1.

Chapter Six

1. Wollstonecraft, Mary. *A Vindication of the Rights of Women.* 1792. In Carol McPhee and Ann Fitzgerald, *Feminist Quotations: Voices of Rebels, Reformers, and Visionaries.* New York: Thomas Y. Crowell, 1979.

2. Shore, Lesley Irene. *Healing the Feminine.* St. Paul: Llewellyn, 1995.

Chapter Seven

1. "Newsmaker." The New Yorker. *Austin American Statesman,* March 18, 1996.

2. Dowd, Maureen. "Cosmo's winning formula stands up to test of time." The New York Times. *Austin American Statesman,* April 30, 1996.

3. *Ibid.*

4. Goodman, Ellen. "An encouraging note of skepticism on feminism's third wave." Boston Globe. *Austin American Statesman,* July 19, 2003.

5. *Cosmo Girl.* "476 Ways to Look Sexy for Spring," March 2004. New York.

6. Steinem, Gloria. *Revolution from Within.* Boston: Little, Brown and Company, 1992.

7. Johnson, Robert A. *Femininity Lost and Regained.* New York: Harper & Row, 1990, p. 91-92.

8. *Ibid.*

9. Jung, C.G. *Aspects of the Feminine.* Princeton: Princeton University Press, 1982.

10. Sanford, John A. *The Invisible Partners.* New York: Paulist Press, 1980.

11. Lynch, Jerry and Huang, Chungliang Al. *Working Out, Working Within.* New York: Jeremy P. Tarcher/Putnam, 1999, p. 61-62.

Chapter Eight

1. Chisholm, Shirley. *Unbought and Unbossed.* 1970. In Carol McPhee and Ann Fitzgerald, *Feminist Quotations: Voices of Rebels, Reformers, and Visionaries.* New York: Thomas Y. Crowell, 1979.

2. Sue, Derald Wing and Sue, David. *Counseling the Culturally Different.* New York: John Wiley and Sons, 1981. A model for racial/cultural identity development.

3. Atkinson, Donald; Morten, George, and Sue, Derald. *Counseling American Minorities*, 6th ed. New York: McGraw-Hill, 2004, table 2.1, p. 41.

4. Warsh, Sylvia Maultash. "Except for Laura Secord," *Barbed Lyres: Canadian Venomous Verse.* Key Porter Books, 1991. Laura Secord was the one woman studied in Canadian history.

5. Estes, Clarissa Pinkola. *Women Who Run With the Wolves.* New York: Ballantine, 1992.

Chapter Nine

1. Cady, Susan; Ronan, Marian, and Taussig, Hal. *Sophia*. San Francisco: Harper & Row, 1986, p. 18.

2. Bradley, Marion Zimmer. *The Mists of Avalon*. New York: Ballantine Books, 1982, p. x - xi.

3. *Ibid.*, p. x-xi.

4. Eisler, Riane. *The Chalice and the Blade*. San Francisco: Harper, 1988.

5. Johnson, Elizabeth A. *She Who Is: The Mystery of God in Feminist Theological Discourse*. New York: Crossroad, 1997, p. 5.

6. *Ibid.*

7. Kopenec, Stefani G. "Baptists urge end to same-sex partner benefits." Associated Press. *Austin American Statesman,* June 20, 1997.

8. "Gender-Neutral Bible Discontinued." Associated Press, Internet, June 20,1997.

9. Unity School of Christianity. *Wings of Song*. Unity Village, MO: Unity Books, 1984.

10. Johnson, Elizabeth A. *She Who Is: The Mystery of God in Feminist Theological Discourse*. New York: Crossroad, 1997, p. 9.

11. *Ibid.*, p. 9.

12. *Ibid.*

13. *Ibid.*, p. 9.

14. Cady, Susan; Ronan, Marian, and Taussig, Hal. *Sophia.* San Francisco: Harper & Row, 1986.

15. *Ibid.*

16. Engelsman, Joan Chamberlain. *The Feminine Dimension of the Divine.* Wilmette, Illinois: Chiron Publications, 1994.

17. Cady, Susan; Ronan, Marian, and Taussig, Hal. *Sophia.* San Francisco: Harper & Row, 1986, p. 18 - 19.

18. Fox, Matthew. *The Coming of the Cosmic Christ.* San Francisco: Harper and Row, 1988.

19. *Ibid.*, p. 250 - 251.

20. Pagels, Elaine. *The Gnostic Gospels.* New York: Vintage Books, 1981.

21. *Ibid.*

22. *Ibid.*, p. 71.

23. *Ibid.*

24. *Ibid.*, p. xvi.

25. Cleary, Thomas (Ed.). *Immortal Sisters: Secrets of Taoist Women.* Boston: Shambhala, 1989, p. 1.

26. Wing, R.L. *The Tao of Power.* New York: Doubleday, 1986.

27. *Ibid.*

28. Swami Nikhilananda, *The Gospel of Sri Ramakrishna.* New York: Ramakrishna-Vivekananda Center, 1952, p. 38.

29. Wideman, John Edgar. "Russell Means," *Modern Maturity,* Sept-Oct 1995, p. 70.

30. *Ibid.*, p. 70.

31. *Ibid.*, p. 70.

32. Reilly, Patricia Lynn. *A God Who Looks Like Me: Discovering a Woman-Affirming Spirituality.* New York: Ballantine Books, 1995, p. 247.

33. *Ibid.*

34. Morphew, Clark. "Author finds churches close doors on women." *Austin American Statesman,* March 2,1996.

35. White, Victor. *Soul and Psyche: An Enquiry Into the Relationship of Psychotherapy and Religion.* London: Harvill Press, 1960, p. 122-123.

36. Flowers, Betty S. "Mary and Martha," *Extending the Shade.* Plain View Press: Austin, Texas, 1990.

Chapter Ten

1. Adapted from Waley, Arthur. *The Way and Its Power*. New York: Grove Weidenfeld, 1958, p. 178.

2. Lerner, Gerda. *The Creation of Patriarchy*. New York: Oxford Press, 1986.

3. Athanassakis, Apostolos N. *The Homeric Hymns*. Baltimore: The John Hopkins University Press, 1976, p. 3.

4. *Ibid.*

5. Tarn, Nathaniel. *The Persephones*. Santa Barbara, CA: Christopher's Books, 1972. The Second Persephone, The Sixth Persephone.

6. Athanassakis, Apostolos N. *The Homeric Hymns*. Baltimore: The John Hopkins University Press, 1976, p. 4.

7. *Ibid.*, p. 10.

8. *Ibid.*, p. 10.

9. *Ibid.*

10. Gibran, Kahlil. *The Prophet*. New York: Alfred A Knopf, 1963, p. 76.

Appendix

What Do Women Really Want?

Myths are for reflecting and teaching. In that spirit, the following questions are designed to help you know your hag.

• What does your hag look like? (Close your eyes and see if you can conjure her up. You might be surprised. Then draw her or write a physical description of her.)

• Write about her destructive patterns. Her fears. Her anger. Her rage.

What does she want?

How is she trying to get your attention?

How is she subservient to your masculine/animus?

Consider marrying her and giving her a place in your life. What feelings come up for you?

How might you be changed if you accepted her?

• Write to your hag. Holding her image in your mind, tell her what you know about her. Switch hands and let her write back to you.

• Draw, paint, or sculpture your hag. Listen to her words and feelings as you do so.

Figure Three: Vierge Ouvrante Open

To contact the author, go to:

www.feminineconnection.com

www.gayleowens.com

Lightning Source UK Ltd.
Milton Keynes UK
26 November 2009